Shattered Dreams
&
Scorpions at Midnight

a search for sanctuary

Tales from Turkey Volume One

by Miriam McGuirk

mPowr Publishing

First Published in Great Britain 2015 by
mPowr (Publishing) Ltd.

www.mpowrpublishing.com
www.mpowrunlimited.com

A catalogue record for this book is available from the British Library

ISBN – 978-1-907282-63-8

Cover Design & Illustrations by Martyn Pentecost
mPowr Publishing 'Clumpy™' Logo by e-nimation.com
Clumpy™ and the Clumpy™ Logo are trademarks of mPowr Ltd.

To

My wise Turkish family

and

My darling husband Chris

Acknowledgements

There was the *I* when I sat in silence in my writing cave—with a wish to complete Shattered Dreams and Scorpions at Midnight, Volume One.

In order to publish this book the *I* became *We*, thanks to partnering with mPowr Publishing. Thanks to Richard Hagen and Martyn Pentecost for encouraging me to raise the bar in my writing. By opening my eyes to what I can achieve with their mentoring I feel confident in writing under my own name, Miriam McGuirk.

Thank you Liz White, of White Word Media, for your immeasurable work and input. Long may you be that diverse and creative angel on my shoulder.

Thank you Richard Torble, head shot and portrait photographer. I love the photograph on the back cover of the book, it has captured the essence of who I have become.

Finally, to my much-loved superhero husband, promoter and manager—You are the best.

Contents

Glossary

A list of Turkish words and phrases found in the book— in order of appearance (marked with a *).

Turkish — Meaning — Pronunciation

Yabanci — foreigner — ya-ban-juh

Merhaba — hello — me-rhaba

Günaydın — good morning — gew-ni-duhn

Nasılsın? — how are you? — nah-ssil-sin

Hanim — wife (in this region of Turkey) — han-em

Hoşgeldiniz — welcome — hosh-geldin-iz

Raki — traditional alcoholic drink (anise flavoured) — ra-ke

Şerefe — cheers — she-r-e-feh

Çay — tea — chay (ch as in church)

Papatya Çay — camomile tea — pah-pah-tya

İyi akşamlar — good evening — iyi ak-sham-lar

Afiyet olsun — eat well — ah-fee-yeht olsoon

Melekler — angels — mell-eck-lair

Cesur — brave — jess-ur

Cihan — a name — gee-han

Cennet — paradise — jen-ett

Yaprak Dolmasi — stuffed vine leaves — yap-rack doll-mass-e

Dolma — stuffed vegetables, e.g. peppers/tomatoes

Gözleme — pancake — guz-le-meh

İnşallah — God willing — in-shal-ah

Köfte — meat balls — kurf-teh

Makarna — pasta — mack-r-na

Şımarık — naughty / spolit — shim-r-ick

Diş Hekimi — dentist —

Baba — father — ba-ba

Kontrol — check — kont-rol

İyi günler — have a good day — iyi-gewn-lehr

Simit/s — circle of bread with sesame topping — sim-eat

Ağabey — elder brother — r-bee

Helva — traditional sweet treat (crystallised paste of nuts and sugar) — hell-vah

How the
Turkish Adventure
Began...

10th April 1997 – 7 p.m. – Work – London

"Miriam, Miriam, are you OK in there? You have been gone for ages..."

Keeled over, head on the floor, knees on cold terracotta tiles, I felt a warm, sticky liquid trickling down the right hand side of my face. I put my right hand up to touch it. In the dark I could not see, but it felt like blood. *Tap-tap-tap* on the door again.

"Miriam, for God's sake say something, I am worried about you, open the door."

In a low voice that did not sound like mine I managed to call out, "I have fallen, but I think I am OK." I tried to kneel, holding on to the handbasin. With slow deliberation I managed to pull myself up to standing. A small, round mirror hung on a hook on the back of the door but I could not focus with any detail. Disoriented, I reached for the door handle to open it.

Stella, my work colleague and dearest friend for many years, stepped forward to give me a hug. Shocked, she took my shoulders and exclaimed, "What have you done to yourself? You're bleeding. It looks as if you have cut yourself above the right eye... Miriam you cannot go on like this. We are going to the hospital now to get you checked out."

Through dazed eyes, "No, I'll be fine I want to go home. I'll call CJ and let him know what has happened." I could see deep concern etched on Stella's face. Shakily we linked arms as we made our way from the bathroom door to my office. I reached for my phone and dialled.

CJ picked up, "Hi M, what's up?" Emotions running high, I started to cry down the line.

Somehow I managed to convey my predicament, "I have collapsed again, I am driving straight home. Can you ask Doctor Keogh to come to the house please?"

Stella offered to drive me.

"I'll be grand," I said, "really, I shall take my time."

"Not before you have drunk a large cup of sweet tea and stopped shaking, you do know you could be concussed?" She wagged her finger at me. Reluctantly, she walked me to my car; I got in and smiled a cheery wave. I did not feel cheery, I felt weak with a yearning to lie down and sleep for a long time. I have no idea how I guided the gears and wheels but I arrived safely. CJ ran to open the door. I lurched forward. He caught me, hugged me.

There waiting solemnly in the lounge was the tall, youthful-looking doctor. Dr. Keogh was empathetic but firm, "Miriam you have ignored my warnings and advice. Tomorrow I will speak to some consultants, set up appointments for you to have some tests. We will take it a step at a time. Whether you like it or not, you are grounded until further notice. Spelling it out Miriam, you stay in bed, you rest, sleep all day if you need to. Your situation is now critical."

Stella was right; I could not go on living in this way. It was the first time in twenty years a doctor had taken an interest in my health. Feelings of relief washed over me, finally I could let go and allow myself to fall whatever the outcome. Tests were done, operations (all five of them, small but significant) were booked and completed.

Still grounded and bewildered by what was

happening I was an emotional and physical mess. Sore, in pain, dispirited, one morning Dr. Keogh appeared at the house.

"Miriam I wish to share information about your ongoing health issues. With the completed ops the scars will heal in time. I don't want to add to your anxieties but I need you to listen and hear what I have to say. You have M.E.—Myalgic Encephalopathy—the worst case scenario I have ever seen, due to the fact it took so long to get a positive professional diagnosis."

Brushing his words off in disbelief I said, "Sorry, did I hear you correctly Doctor, are you saying I have M.E.? Surely not, I really do not have time for this illness."

"My dear Miriam this is not going to go away with a flick of your hand or you dismissing my words. I urge you not to fight it please, you have sabotaged your body for years with sleep deprivation, your immune system is shot to pieces, many of your vital organs are closing down, I could go on. We will get you through this if you work with me. Acceptance is key, it is going to take all the time it needs to."

He left. I felt numb, his words going round and round in my head. I did not really take them in or understand how I needed to change, to stop and finally *be*.

Sadly Dr. Keogh was diagnosed with Crohn's disease shortly after that and resigned from medicine. I felt abandoned and isolated.

Life changed forever as I became the wilting plant in a pot stuck in one place looking out at the world, as it walked around me or passed me by including close friends and some family too.

This was the beginning of the end of my working career as I had known it for over twenty-four years. I went into a spiral of boom and bust hoping complementary practitioners would provide the miracle cure or that Dr Keogh's medical colleagues could weave their magic and fix me, put me back together like you would stitch up the old, raggedy teddy bear you have loved since you were a child. Oh how I hankered to have my life back, but it seemed like an elusive butterfly.

CJ, puzzled and thrown by his new wife's condition (six months into our marriage), would leave early each morning to head to his office in the West End with a smile and a "Have a great day darling," as I lay mummy-like on my back, swaddled in sheets and sleep-deprived. Eventually, I extracted myself from the sheets to head downstairs to make breakfast—a test of time and effort. CJ would come home in the evenings to find me in the same position, in bed, with a "So what have you been up to today?"

My bright beacon of light and hope came in the form of Stella who visited bringing with her tasty food morsels, uplifting classical music and many stories of her turbulent love life. Stella was petit, curvy, tousled blonde curls, high heels and full, pouty, red lips. She was a food and beverage manager, a people person who loved her job as I did. Outside of work and her sombre black suit and white shirt her alter ego was Marilyn Monroe, with hair and make-up to match, straight from the set of her adored Hollywood actress.

One morning Stella knocked on the front door. "What does a gal have to do round here to get a decent cup of coffee and a poached egg on toast?" she shouted through the letter box. It saved energy if I threw the keys out the window. She unlocked the door and let herself in. I could smell her heady perfume (yes, it was Chanel No. 5), far too pungent for this hour as she cast her spell fluttering like a butterfly around the house. Classical music resonated through the floorboards with the smell of coffee brewing and fresh bread toasting wafting up the stairs into my bedroom. Stella appeared in the doorway in her inimitable way. "Rise and shine, dearest Miriam. Let me tempt you with a scrummy breakfast. Later I shall help you shower and with my expert bang-on-trend hairdryer I will style your hair and apply some glam make up. You will feel more upbeat and able to face a better day." She willed me to be positive.

"Oh Stella not today, I just want to lie here," I whispered.

"Sorry M, but if the other M was here she would not approve of you falling into CJ's tracky bottoms and billowing sweatshirt each day with the heavy fabric swallowing you up. Looks like you have decided to enter the 'Mini-Michelin-Woman Contest', and at this moment there is every chance you will win. This is not a good look Miriam, it is so not you. What happened to the glamorous and ritzy style everyone admired, with never a hair or eyelash out of place?"

"I have lost it," I replied, "it is simply too much effort."

"Don't be ridiculous, Ms. Boop-Boop-Be-Do, whether you like it or not I am here to stay and support you. Over breakfast we can talk about your progress, what the supposed professionals are doing to help you and your condition. M, in Marilyn's wise words, 'Sometimes things fall apart so that better things can fall together.'

"Remember M, I am here to help you put the pieces of the new jigsaw of your life back together."

"Ah so sweet and kind, thank you Stella." I shed a few more tears.

I sat on the stairs and pushed myself down on my derrière one step at a time.

As we finished our breakfast I discussed with Stella the latest lack-of-help bulletin. "The scientific professionals do not know what to do with me apart from issuing prescriptions for depression, sleeping tablets, and telling me to 'go and have a nice life'. Frustrated and angry does not begin to describe how I feel right now Stella. A few mornings ago, with every ounce of energy I could muster, I sat in the consulting rooms in front of the bulkily-padded female GP at this Centre of Excellence...

Dr. Gubby leaned across her desk, "Have you thought about exercise my dear? Perhaps some swimming or walking will help with your all-round fitness. Oh, and don't forget to keep some dry biscuits in your back pocket and pace dear, that's it, keep pacing."

"Can you believe it, I was dismissed again—job done, a complete recovery imminent." I started to shake with emotion and bless Stella's patience as she sat and listened, holding my hand with such empathy.

Stella was indignant. "M, this is appalling coming from a doctor; it seems to me they have no idea or interest in you. You have been the fittest gal I know, always taking part in some form of sport or outdoor activity never mind the number of workouts you did each week at the gym. I have a good mind to go down to the surgery to ask Dr. Gubby, 'And tell me Doctor do you practise what you preach to my friend Miriam and take heed of your own advice? How do you feel this is working for you?' Hummph."

By the year 2000 there was no improvement. I woke up one morning and threw some of my tablets into the big, green bin at the side of the house and flushed the remainder down the toilet. This was my secret as I set about researching every aspect of M.E. Step by step I started to create a more structured life with natural supplements, an energising organic diet and some gentle exercise.

One day a more tuned-in complementary practitioner, Sally, suggested "Miriam check out south-western Turkey, the mountains of Portugal, or even India. They have been proven to help some people with this condition." I saw a glimmer of light shimmering down the dark tunnel I was living in. On arrival home I discussed Sally's suggestions with CJ.

CJ played devil's advocate: "Miriam, how the hell would you make that challenging journey to India for the clean air and natural environment of the Himalayan mountains for months on end, isolated, perhaps with people you may not wish to be with? Is the climate in Portugal so different from the UK?"

Mulling it over I scrapped the notion of becoming a nomad, with a tent and some food cans hanging from my back to trek across India, to heal in the Himalayas. I also decided to give the lakes and forests of Portugal a miss too.

July 2001

One evening an animated CJ arrived home from work, "We are going to have our first holiday together, we are going to south-west Turkey." Excitedly he waved two tickets in the air and then wrapped his arms around me. "We are going to get you to the sun, to the sea. You love swimming, maybe, just maybe, a warmer environment will help you. I don't know how but by God we are going to get you there. That is my promise. M, you remember Jeff my textile friend, he raves about this area. He has holidayed there six times with his family. It's booked, it's organised, all you have to do is think nice thoughts of being by the sea there and pack... easy." When I saw the tickets and heard what CJ was planning I went into total meltdown. I panicked every time I looked at the calendar—the date of departure loomed in front of me.

Two days after 9/11, with anxieties running high, feeling shattered, nerves frayed, even forgetting to bring my current passport to the airport (it was eventually delivered in time thanks to a kindly neighbour), somehow we boarded the plane heading east.

September 2001 – Day 4 at 8 a.m. – South-West Turkey

"Come on M, come on darling, only a few metres

more and you are there."

"I can do this." I said it out loud, putting one foot in front of the other.

"I tell you what, I'll give you a piggyback to the edge, then you are on your own." CJ encouraged me. He dropped me down gently into the lapping water, "Just do it, go swim," he smiled. Walking cautiously on the soft silky sand, I went deeper and deeper until the water was up to my hips. "Don't forget to breathe!" I heard CJ call out as I put my head into the calm millpond. I stretched my body out to its full five-foot-four-and-a-bit length, with one arm out, then the other, pushing back, then, with a kick-kick-kick of my feet I relaxed into the flow of the crawl. The refreshing water on my skin made it tingle. Underwater, I was in harmony with the seabed.

I felt powerful for the first time in years.

"I did it! I did it!" I cried out as I came up for air. CJ followed behind me. The horizon ahead was a tranquil haze, the heat of the sun slowly burning it off. I turned onto my back and floated, letting every muscle, every sinew and body part relax. I lay suspended in my own flotation tank, looking up at the rich blue sky. "Wow, I feel alive, I am swimming after all these years, I have dreamed of this day. Thank you CJ for making it happen."

Squealing with laughter and delight I was a child again: splish-splashing arms and legs in the sheer joy of floating without armbands. For the next half hour I swam, remembering all the strokes I had spent years perfecting, soaking up the energy of the sea.

"I want to become a dolphin or a mermaid," I

called out, "to live in harmony with this healing water, swim all day, be stroked and get fed by friendly folks who pass by in their boats." It was time to get out of the water, I raised my fist in the air with a whoop-whoop-I-feel-amazing sound. We made our way back to the apartment to shower. I was ready to eat a well-deserved power breakfast. Feeling relaxed I sat on the whitewashed terrace looking out to miles of creamy white sandy beach and crystal clear water.

While we ate CJ remarked, "M, I cannot remember when I last saw you smiling, laughing, happy. You need more of this miracle healing, we have ten more days to move you forward on this positive new track."

Later, lying on the beach on a chaise longue with a woven umbrella for shade, I drifted in and out of a luxurious restoring sleep. I had taken another step in my recovery.

That holiday was pivotal in helping me realise that perhaps I could nurture a quality life. One that worked for me.

Over the next two years I spent a total of fifteen weeks in south-west Turkey. I rented a small house near the lapping water from my new friend Deniz. Her parents owned a hotel with views directly onto the beach. We connected from day one, her fireball of energy—vivacious with a sense of fun—helping me to experience and learn to live in her eastern culture. I spent quiet days at her house in a natural, warm environment. During each visit my energy levels improved.

Excited, I knew it was time to make some real, life-changing decisions...

Sea and Solitude

Summer of 2003

With a big leap of faith CJ and I boarded a plane to Turkey. Taking a few deep breaths I put my hand in his and said, "Here we go, this is our moment, no going back." I leaned into his shoulder for reassurance as we took off.

Owls follow us wherever we go...

Since childhood CJ has loved owls; they follow him wherever he travels and they have become our sign of good luck.

Arriving at dawn in the stillness of the early morning, interrupted by the clacking sound of the taxi's diesel engine, the driver unloaded our cases. Standing on the narrow path by the entrance to our gated house the scent of jasmine filled the air. Linking arms we walked up the steps to our front door.

"This is the cusp of change, darling CJ," I spoke softly. Through the calm of the morning light two owls hooted, perched on a window ledge opposite our house. "Surely this is a good omen." I looked at CJ, emotions running high at the prospect of a healthier chapter in both our lives.

We woke early the next morning to the sound of melodious birdsong. I pushed open the window shutters of our bedroom and the doors out to the marbled terrace that encircled the house. Before me were picture-postcard views of bright azure skies and rolling green hills. "Come on, you!" I called back to CJ who was hiding under the covers, "It's time for our initiation ceremony into this new life." We headed to the beach, some five-hundred metres away, CJ pulling me along as I struggled—brain foggy, body oh-so-tired. Determined, I submerged myself into the healing sea as it wrapped itself around me. Slowly the salty, clear water worked its magic, I came alive.

"This is pure bliss, my morning routine from now on," I called out. "This is like our private beach where I can do yoga stretches on these large, healing, white stones right here at the water's edge."

Back at the house I unpacked boxes, one by one, that had eventually arrived by container from the UK via the port city of Izmir—some three-and-a-half hours away by road.

My new Turkish friend Deniz (who was introduced to me by the tour operator on our first visit) said, "Miriam, what do you say if my housekeeper helps you a few days a week? I trust her; she has worked with my mother and myself for a few years. She will do whatever you ask around the house, she will even work in the garden. Her name is Cihan*, shall I speak with her?" A few days later Deniz drove to the house with Cihan and introduced us. Cihan was a young, traditional girl with brown, puppy-wide eyes of wonder as she gazed at the yabanci* with the funny accent. Bashful, with no English and only a desire to help, she worked tirelessly and between us we started to create the feel of our new home.

Heady days ran into months as we put roots down. We felt we were half-tourists/half-natives living in amongst this quiet, scattered Turkish community.

Workmen came and went, finishing the painting of the house whenever it suited them it seemed. One such morning CJ called me from his office some twenty minutes away, "The builder has confirmed the painters will be with you shortly to varnish the verandas and paint the door frames white. No need to get involved, just carry on." He hung up. By three in the afternoon, with not even a single painter on my doorstep, I headed to rest.

Within half an hour I heard a man shouting up at the window of my bedroom. "Is there anybody here? Let us in." Groggy, I went down two narrow flights of marble stairs to open the front door. You have heard of buses arriving all at the same time... well, a team of five men stood on the veranda armed with plastic pots of paint, varnish and brushes and dressed in their grubby, paint-stained overalls. The leader pushed past me and ordered the others to go and finish the work the builder had requested.

Superfluous to any requirements or conversation I followed him. "As you are several hours late, I am resting in my bedroom. Apologies but you will have to work around me if necessary." Leader man nodded. The men streamed in and out, onto the veranda huffing and puffing, averting their eyes with embarrassment. I did not care, I needed to sleep. To avoid eye contact I pulled on my eye mask, thinking positive thoughts. Late in the afternoon I removed it, relieved the workers were gone. However they had left their dirty evidence behind: cardboard and empty paint pots were strewn across the garden, never to be cleared unless I did the job.

I examined their work only to find the marbled terraces on the three floors covered with drips of white paint and varnish. I was none too pleased with the results but, for now, I was glad solitude was restored at mine.

By midsummer with temperatures and humidity soaring our neighbourhood came alive with Istanbulians arriving in the early hours, cars packed with people and provisions. The summer party was coming to town, starting from early morning. Women would shout orders at their husbands, "Get up, get up, it's time to take the children to swim. Hurry, hurry, the children are waiting for you," as they bundled the unenthusiastic men out the door with towels and swimming paraphernalia. The women shouted at each other from across their terraces with good mornings, swapping food or chitter-chatter about their lazy, hungover husbands. They noisily bashed their rugs with a big brush throwing them over the side to air whilst Turkish music beat out at full volume. The daily hosing down of the terraces followed, then setting tables in the shade for the families' return to eat a late breakfast. Later the sound of children's laughter would fill the air as they played and rode bicycles in the bright sunshine.

We sat quietly in the shade of our veranda, eating breakfast, allowing this high-energy activity to move around us. Before I could even take my first sip of coffee inquisitive neighbours hung by their doors or from their open windows and called across to us, "Welcome, welcome, you are new here. Merhaba, günaydın*, nasılsın*?"

Some mornings these women would run across to ours still in their rollers, nightdresses and flip-flops to present us with gifts of food. "Please take this hot bread just baked and this is fruit from my trees." Grateful for the hospitality and the warm welcome to their world of food, sun, sea and loud chatter they were not the peaceful, healing mornings I had wished for after my initial beach and yoga therapy.

One evening, in a hail of busyness and ceremony, a family arrived in a shiny new Mercedes. They were met by the couple who maintained the communal areas. Why, they almost bowed to this man as they helped him unload his full car. He shouted at the couple, checking everything was in place at his house just as he wished, before dismissing them with not even a thank you.

Uninvited, one by one, this newly-arrived family appeared at the entrance to our house the next morning. They walked onto our terrace each pulling up a chair to sit with us.

"Hello, Merhaba. So you are the newly arrived foreigners, welcome to your new home. We hope you will be happy here. We come from a big city near the Black Sea in northern Turkey. I am Neglin, this is my husband Serjan and these are our children." Two blonde teenagers, a boy and a girl, nodded with warm friendly smiles, Emre and Yasmin. "I have retired this summer as a head teacher in my city school," said the pale-faced, bespectacled and permed Neglin. We shook hands and offered them tea which they accepted. Serjan was a ruddy-faced man, overweight, his breathing laboured. He seemed surly and did not speak English. His weasel eyes darted from side to side when he spoke as he asked question after question in a booming voice, demanding that Neglin translate.

"The children are learning English in school, we can visit each morning to practise speaking with you. In exchange we will guide you with your

Turkish, especially your grammar," Neglin offered.

CJ thanked them for their visit and stood up, "It is time for me to head off for my day."

A barrage of questions followed from inquisitive Serjan, "What is your work? Where is your office? Why did you come to Turkey?" He ignored me and only referred to Neglin as 'hanim*', which is the Turkish for wife. As a Western woman I found that insulting, but CJ gave me a warning look not to say a word.

Serjan materialised most days. Lost in my morning of writing or engrossed in other activities I almost jumped out of my skin each time he appeared in the arched window of my office with his gravelly voice ringing in my sensitive ears. "Hello, I am checking your new front door. What wood are these French windows made from? Where did you buy this special glass?" Always asked gruffly. No morning greeting for me the foreigner.

"As if he owned the place..." I could hear my grandmother's voice from childhood. She did not encourage unannounced guests while she was working.

He would walk into our kitchen uninvited. "Who made your kitchen units and doors?" He pulled them in and out, checking the springs and how they closed. "How much did you pay for this house? What are you spending on this redevelopment?" He slammed one of my kitchen units shut, nearly taking it off its hinges and his finger with it.

I wanted to tell him, "Please leave and stop snooping around our house." Instead, I changed the subject. I did not appreciate his constant popping up but thought it was his way of giving us his approval into this Turkish community.

Initially sweet Yasmin would gently knock on my door at midday, "Miriam, I am here to learn English, can we make conversation? My father has requested you come to dinner one evening that suits you and CJ. We wish to welcome you to our country and the Turkish way of life." I thanked her but my thought was to eat peaceful dinners à deux at ours.

The following week, after much cajoling and out of respect for our neighbours, we walked over to Serjan's home. It was set behind ours and was European in style unlike our more traditionally built Turkish house. Tall Roman-style pillars with roaring alabaster lions graced the double-gated entrance. Inside the décor was bright and garish with opulent gold-trimmed chairs and furniture. Crystal lights hung off-centre, lights one might normally find in a five-star Turkish hotel.

"Hoşgeldiniz*!" Serjan came to the door to greet us with open arms and kissed CJ on each cheek calling him brother. He even shook my hand and smiled, "CJ, you are a lucky man to have a young, intelligent wife."

We made our way onto the back terrace lit up with strip lighting and in this brightness I became aware of Serjan's fox-red hair dye and a comb-over to cover his bald pate. His eyebrows and thick moustache were the same shade of henna. His ruddy face (as if doused in a pot of the wrong shade of blusher) clashed with the red dye, giving him a shine and a mad look. I tried not to stare or laugh. We ate fresh fish grilled on their open barbecue with bowls of colourful salads followed by a platter of thick wedges of red-fleshed water melon—another contrast to Serjan's foxy hair and pink face. The children sat excitedly with us as we interacted in half-Turkish / half-English.

We happily drank water; later Serjan appeared with a smile and a bottle of raki*.

"I have been saving this bottle for a special occasion," he proudly announced. He generously poured the strong stuff for CJ and himself. They added water and it turned white. Serjan stood up "Here's to our new neighbours, to friendship and life at the beach this summer." He saluted each of us with a Şerefe* (cheers) while Neglin and I drank calming Papatya Çay*.

As we walked back to our house I expressed my concerns to CJ, "As Serjan has chosen to call you 'brother' does this mean, darling husband, you will be tempted to change from your silver-squirrel natural hair colour to his tawny red fox look? Why, you could become twins by default!" I laughed.

"Perish the thought," said CJ, laughing too.

Within weeks of the mass arrival of the city folk my sacrosanct time at the beach was intruded upon. Serjan made his daily mandatory checks to mine and to his friends' houses. At six each evening, to cool down, he would hold court either on his mat sitting on the stony beach or he would swim with a childish kind of stroke out to form a circle with his cronies in the sea. In waters deep his booming voice reverberated back onto the beach. His neighbours nodded in agreement as he expounded on whatever subject he chose to have an opinion on. Neglin, with a baseball hat to protect her from the sun, swam separately with the wives forming another circle of conversation. Once back on dry land she waved Merhaba or İyi akşamlar* and walked with her rattan beach mat to sit beside me. There was a vulnerability about her.

"Since Serjan sold his engineering business he continues to fill his time, he likes being involved," she explained.

'Tell me about it!' I thought to myself and prayed that our plum and lemon along with the newly planted olive trees would grow tall and leafy with super speed, allowing us some privacy, ensuring it was more challenging for the unfit Serjan to climb over the wall. Would placing some wire along the top be too much of a statement to tell him to back off with his daily visits? I was tempted to do it anyway.

"Now I understand," I said politely, "he pops up over our wall daily and walks into my house when I am working."

"Oh that's just Serjan's way. He likes to know what his neighbours are up to especially as you are foreigners, you do things differently in your Western world. He enjoys anything to do with buildings," she laughed.

"Then why did you, being Turkish, build a Western-style house while we the foreigners are living in a traditional Turkish house?" I asked.

"Serjan likes to show off and boast about our summer home being the biggest on this estate. It is testament to his success. When you are married to a strong disciplined man for many years Miriam I suppose I simply follow his way and how he likes things done. Be grateful you are not part of our family as he likes to run both our houses and us with military precision."

"Miriam, in truth I feel lost now that my career

in teaching is over. I do not know what I will do after our summer here." She hugged her knees to her chest and rocked back and forth lost in those thoughts. My heart lurched in sympathy at such honesty.

The men, without excuse, would scarper off to play backgammon in-between visits to the beach. At nine o'clock each night the families would gather on their terraces to eat dinner while we, the foreigners who ate earlier, would take a walk once the temperatures started to drop. We were constantly interrupted by "İyi akşamlar, come, come join us," asked by our friendly neighbours.

Politely we replied, "Thank you we have eaten. We wish you a good meal and a happy evening," walking at a faster pace to get away. Tired of repeating the same greeting we started to walk a different route to avoid these nightly invites. By ten the disco balls were hung from the corrugated ceiling in the gazebo-like communal social area. The women would make tea in the little kitchen and bring home-made cakes and baklava.

Abba's *Dancing Queen* or the famous Turk, Tarkan, with his sexy rendition of *Kiss* would screech out from a battered, old sound system accompanied by flashing disco lights. Women, dressed-up, made-up and bejewelled, would swing and sway as they cavorted across the gazebo floor with a little wiggle to attract their husbands' attention. It had no effect on the men, who were oblivious, sitting at square plastic tables playing their much-loved backgammon, betting their money spurred on by many a glass of raki.

The women, on seeing me pass by, would reach

out to drag me into their circle, "Let us teach you how we dance to this music." They would laugh playfully, "CJ, go and sit with the men. You can learn how to play backgammon Turkish way."

It may have been disrespectful to decline their offers. Perhaps we were putting distance between us and them... time would tell, it was still early days at their summer retreat.

Serjan was often in the centre of this serious game playing and drinking while Neglin wisely returned home to read.

Raucous banter, laughter and singing would often continue until after midnight when wives dragged their monosyllabic, drunken husbands back to their houses with lots of "Shh, shh! You will wake our neighbours..." Sometimes I awoke in the early hours to what I thought was the sound of logs being sawed but, in reality, it was the snorting, hissing sounds of the men as they lay unconscious in their beds, their snores echoing from the open windows of their bedrooms across to us.

One steamy, hot evening over dinner I said to CJ, "Is this the healing quiet life we were hoping for? Loud voices crashing and banging sounds all day long just like being in a city. There are days when I feel overwhelmed, it reminds me of some black comedy where our neighbours are the players and we the audience. Every night we watch the same show go round and round like the merry-go-round. I feel exposed with no privacy, we are being constantly observed and monitored. I am tired of our house being an open house. The only time I am alone is when I am enveloped in the sea. I feel sad and disappointed." I hung my head in frustration, tired and oh, so weary...

"Hmmmm... so what do we do now?" CJ asked as he hugged me.

Shortly after that emotional evening with CJ a little miracle happened.

One evening, as I bounced on my mini trampoline on the roof terrace, there below me were the Istanbulian party animals packing up to make that long drive back to their city that never sleeps. I bounced for joy calling out, "Thank you! Thank you to the skies, miracles do happen."

Relief washed over me, Serjan was also closing up his house for the summer as Neglin prepared to drive beyond Istanbul to the colder Black Sea area. The glitter ball season was finally at an end. It was time for me to celebrate with a little solitary dance on my terrace.

There are Many Illnesses

The following April, as the temperatures rose, Serjan and Neglin suddenly arrived back from the Black Sea. They of the purring, silver-metallic Mercedes were followed by a truck filled with an army of workers, a Portakabin and a few tents. What was he planning to do?

The familiar, gravelly voice of Serjan barked orders from early morning until late at night to his crew of men. This became the order of each day.

Neglin came to mine bearing food gifts, "So you did not go back to the UK for the winter months?" She seemed surprised.

"No, we remained at the house," I replied. "Why?"

"Oh, Serjan has been scheming these last months; he says he wants to spend more time by the sea. He is determined to make changes and has decided to build more modern aspects to our house, just like yours. He's insisting I have a new kitchen even though my old one works perfectly well. He continues for some reason although there is no reason to develop our house into more of a showpiece—bigger and better than his neighbours' and friends'. He will not listen to my reasoning of 'Why?'"

She sighed a deep sigh of resignation.

I was alone one evening planning to relax, my doors were firmly closed, and I had only a candle for light. My finger was on the play button ready to watch a film. My heart leapt at an impatient rat-a-tat-tat on the front door. Reluctantly I pushed myself out of my chair and padded across the room to open it.

Before me stood a young woman, wailing, "My

worst nightmare has come to pass. Oh Miriam... you will not believe who has come to stay at our house."
I ushered the hysterical Deniz into the lounge and made some restoring çay. Then I guided her to a comfy chair while I sat opposite and held her hand. I waited to hear of some horrendous catastrophe.

Deniz, almost choking as she sipped the çay in between gulps of air, had tears running down her smeared face. "Zecki has been ill, sneezing, with a temperature and sore throat. Feeling sorry for himself, alone in the house while I was at work, he telephoned his mother asking her to come and take care of him.

He explained it away with a 'You are working and cannot take time off, my mother knows what to do, I need her here.'"

Normally a strong, vivacious lady, Deniz, supports her friends, copes with running the home and looks after her husband, all while working at her parents' hotel in the nearest town. This night she was a mess.

"Miriam, within twenty-four hours MIL (mother-in-law) appeared from Istanbul to take up residence at my home to look after her little boy... Yes, my thirty-something husband, the big-shot solicitor, all six-foot-four, strapping, muscle-bound, honed-and-toned Zecki."

She shook her head in disbelief. "I never knew him to be a wimp."

I listened to her tale with sympathy.

"I am in such a dilemma of having to deal with my mother-in-law. We are a couple from a modern city, what the hell is Zecki thinking? Now the fun has really started. Miriam, I am not joking, Sevinc feels that no daughter-in-law knows how to take care of her sick boy. Mummy's way is the only way to help her son recuperate and get back on his feet again."

"What am I going to do?" she asked me, the foreigner.

It was not my place to give advice. How I view the world and deal with family situations would not bode well for her or her mother-in-law. I poured her another glass of çay while she offloaded her burden.

I had previously met Zecki's mother when I first came to Turkey. She was a small, chiselled woman with tight, wavy, ash-blonde hair—her posture rigid, her manner cool. When we met she was formal, "I am Sevinc, glad to meet you Miriam. Zecki and Deniz have spoken about you fondly. Welcome to our country and life here. As you see it is different to how you live in the UK, I hope you will be happy and able to make the necessary adjustments."

And that was that. She did not naturally do small talk and it was clear she did not wish to take our relationship any further. Each time I met her she was distant and polite and was always dressed in a uniform of severe black, brown or grey. She wore narrow constricted skirts which went below the knee and practical velcro-fastening shoes or sandals. She never wore any make-up. When she spoke about her much-loved son the intensity manifested itself as a pulse on her right cheek that twitched as her eyes lit up. Of humour, there was none, just a sadness that cast a shadow across her face and her body language.

After I met Sevinc, Deniz updated me on Zecki's family history. "Zecki is an only son without a father. Sevinc lost her husband when he was a young boy.

Mother and son have clung to each other until I came along and stole him away, according to her."

As we sat sipping çay Deniz continued to vent her spleen. "Miriam, while I was at work MIL arrived and assigned herself the largest guest bedroom. I have been ushered into the small spare room with the single bed. MIL has placed another single bed in her beloved son's room for emergencies, 'Just in case he needs me during the night,' she claims. Grant me patience and help me keep my mouth shut!" Deniz looks up to the ceiling, appealing to the powers that be.

After that drama Deniz sneaked over to mine every other evening for reassurance, my warm lounge a space for her to let go as she imparted her tales of what was happening at sickbay.

In between the escapades of Zecki's mother and his drawn-out illness I was dealing with my own situation of illness—I named it *A Man Possessed or was that Obsessed?*

"Neglin, help me please, you and Serjan can do whatever work you like to your house but the noise, the disruption, is becoming intrusive into my daily routine. You know how I have to live and how I need my restful hours, which at the moment are nil."

I lived in hope she could persuade her husband to show a little respect to his new neighbours, even CJ whom he had renamed 'brother' the previous summer.

One morning I popped over to chat with Neglin. She stood by her newly-installed outdoor kitchen washing up dishes in her garden in yellow marigolds.

"I am aware how Serjan wishes to complete this project, but, as we live so close to each other is it possible that Serjan could ask the workers to start at eight and finish by six each evening? That way we get to eat a calm breakfast before they arrive and we can sit outside on our terrace to eat dinner without the noise, dust and bright lights." I reasoned with Neglin.

Serjan appeared at his wife's side, his response a disgruntled grunt. Neglin stepped forward, "Of course we can do that, can't we Serjan?" He nodded, but in the days and weeks that followed he carried on working his way and he no longer spoke to me apart from the occasional nod of his red head.

Deniz continued to call around for her sessions of offloading therapy.

"Can you believe it? Sevinc is knitting Zecki a jumper as she props herself up in bed on night watch, claiming she wants him to have an undisturbed night's sleep with no interference from me, his wife. Miriam, I know she means well but this is taking a mother's love too far."

Eventually Deniz left for another night alone in her single bed in the spare room.

With CJ away on business I continued to reassure my Turkish friend with lots of hugs. She was in much need of TLC, her life suddenly turned upside down because of a few snuffles and an obsessive mother. "Does that count as yet another illness?" I asked her?

Deniz was equally sympathetic to my situation, my life became more turbulent and anxiety-driven as each day passed. Serjan had a manic need to turn his house into some sort of castle. Hammering, banging and shouting through layers of thick dust, the noise grew even louder as he extended the working hours of his men until ten at night.

Deniz and I continued our discussions. "Why is it men's illnesses are such high drama and the worst-case scenarios according to them?" Deniz asks another evening. We were resorting to drinking a decent glass of wine—a de-stresser we told ourselves.

I clambered onto my soapbox, "In my western experience, men and illness do not marry well. At the onset of a sniffle, croak in the throat, or a slight wheeze men go into panic mode and become hypochondriacs. I say this with more conviction since living here, Deniz, and especially since hearing about your ongoing soap opera." I was in full flow. "You have probably noticed at times of illness words like, 'Dreadful cold, the ultimate flu, the highest temperature, or a strange and mysterious virus and fever, or I thought I was dying' are thrown in for greatest effect. Believe me dear friend I have been through my own dramas with CJ when, through a blocked nose, the conversation goes...

"'I...'m so ill... du have doe idea, I feel terrible. Aaaaaaachoooo. I have a really high aaaaaaaaaaachooooooo, temperature. Can you make me a hot drink and some ding to eat, peas?'

"Peas," I reply, "you don't like peas. Oh, you mean please. Give me strength! I say quietly to myself."

"Why is it Deniz, that you and I when we are ill do not have a need to go into child speak, cough like wild barking dogs and share our germs with those around us? Selfless to the end, that's us!"

"Angels of mercy and patience," or in Turkish, Melekler*, laughs Deniz. "You are right Miriam, life changes when there is illness about and our men cough and splutter, tossing and turning with no consideration for us. When we were younger it was a passionate fever that kept us awake at night, or so my memory recalls. You want to say, 'Oh for heaven's sake man, pull yourself together, it's a cold get over it...' In reality I have learned to remain calm, with an empathetic voice, "OK darling," because, if I don't, he will tell his mother about the lack of sympathy he is receiving from his wife. At least you do not have to deal with the interference of a mother-in-law living here." We chuckle at the absurdity of Deniz's situation.

"So the question is Deniz, is this a son missing his mother's tender loving care and pampering or is it simply a man's way of looking for even more attention by reverting to childlike behaviour? Look on the positive side—you can escape to work each day." Again I try to reassure her.

"Yes I know, I am grateful for that but, on my return home, I find that not only has Sevinc taken over as chief carer she has also assumed management of my house. She has scrubbed, cleaned, polished and washed my rugs and floor coverings, every centimetre and corner has been checked for possible dust or dirt. I get a full report in the evenings, indeed MIL has even taken to rearranging the furniture. The contents of the cupboards in the kitchen and bathroom and the fridge have all been changed around." Deniz shakes her head in exasperation.

"Miriam, I ask her, 'Why do you need to keep altering and moving my things? I am happy with them as they are."

MIL retorts with indignation, 'I cannot find anything, my way is a better use of space. I am helping you. I know better than anyone how to run my son's house efficiently.'"

"Ouch, that must hurt..." I say to her.

"Yes, my status as wife has become obsolete too." Deniz takes another glug of wine.

Deniz relayed how MIL prepared dinner each evening according to her menus and Zecki's taste. She made daily shopping lists for Deniz to pick up on her way home after work. By the end of the week, Deniz is shattered and irritated beyond reason.

"I feel I am no longer important in Zecki's life," Deniz confides. "I mean how long does it take to knit a jumper and to recover from a cold? Zecki on the other hand is wallowing in his mother's pampering and Sevinc still has him in her grasp and is relishing the time she is spending with her son. Miriam, she will not let go, she is obsessed with him—her claws are firmly entrenched in his mind too. Ultimately I cannot come between a mother and her son unless I want a major division in the family. That said, if this carries on and Zecki continues to allow his mother to press his emotionally-charged buttons, I feel the need to go and live at my parents' hotel for a while. Sevinc can knit as many jumpers as she wants and they can go back to living their old life together." Deniz starts to cry, demented and exhausted.

I pour her another glass of wine

"Best not let him get ill too often," I say. "Look on the bright side, maybe the barometer for Sevinc is when the jumper is finished she will leave knowing Zecki is recovered and warm in his new chunky knit. At least she is not living permanently across the hall or next door to you. You'll get back on track again. Zecki loves you, he has told me many times; you are his world." I say this whilst keeping my toes, feet and fingers crossed.

I may never understand this need men seem to have for ongoing mothering as they grow into middle age but I have to accept this is the way it is in parts of Turkey. As one Turkish friend explained his view on this sensitive subject, "My love for my wife is immeasurable, but my love for my mother is endless. We have come from our mother's womb and we will return to her always."

And so it is, life's rich tapestry of men, mothers and obsessive illnesses go merrily on their way until the next drama.

In the meantime Serjan needed sorting out with his desire to be king of the castle. He continued his mission—a man possessed—to make his house bigger and better, and Neglin let him.

I spoke to the manager who oversaw all areas to do with the running of the estate, "Efe we need your help, we are at our wits' end with Serjan's behaviour in extending and modernising his house. You must hear the hammering and banging too? He has his workers on site from early morning until ten at night." I appealed to his normally helpful Turkish nature. "Surely as one of his own, you and he have been friends for a many a year, you can appeal to him to be more aware of his quiet neighbours. I am sure if you speak with him he will listen to your reasoning?"

Efe sympathised and shrugged, "Serjan is a bit of a bully, his way is the only way, and we find it is best not to cross him. Did you know he had a triple bypass operation two years ago? His personality has changed since then." And with that no further help was forthcoming as Efe, with Serjan's group of long-standing city friends, drank raki and played backgammon late into the nights.

What to do next? When we first arrived I had caught a glimpse of the life we could have, the opportunity for me to recover by the sea. Was it now lost?

Waxing Warrior

Beep-beep, beep-beep, Turkish pop music blasted from speakers. I walked out to the veranda and waved to my friend Deniz.

"Turn that racket down," I mouthed to her.

She was bouncing in her seat to the sounds of the beat, in sparkling form. "Hurry up" she called out, "I said be ready by ten o'clock."

My neighbour from the Black Sea appeared to check the commotion at mine through her fog of noise, men and dust.

"It's OK Neglin, it's my friend, we are heading off now." I climbed up into Deniz's husband's four-wheel-drive car.

"What has you so perky and dressed up today Missy?" I asked.

"Well Zecki is away for a week, I have borrowed his car, and my parents have insisted I take time off too." Deniz tears up the dirt track onto the main road.

I was happy she was back on track after the long illness debacle and coping with her mother-in-law for weeks on end.

"So Deniz tell me do, did Zecki ever wear his mother's illness jumper? The one Sevinc spent nights hand knitting for her fave son?"

"Miriam you must promise never to mention this if Sevinc is around." It has ended up as a blanket for our dog's basket—she loves it—it was far too big and stretchy for Zecki."

We giggled.

Deniz changed the subject. "I have a surprise for you today," she laughed, "you will thank me for this."

"Hmmm... Any clues as to where are we

heading?" I asked, knowing how impish Deniz can be without her husband's company.

"Ha ha, you will just have to wait and see." She threw back her head with its thick mane of Titian hair and laughed. Within twenty minutes we arrived in a dusty side street and parked by a small shop with blinds on the front windows. An overhead sign read *Burcu's Hair-Coiffeur Salon.* "Miriam, this is your surprise, you are booked in for all that you need waxed this morning."

"But I don't need to be waxed," I protested.

"Unlike you of light hair, we Turkish women of dark hair and skin—and I'm not just talking about what is on the top of our heads or above our eyes—we have a lot of fuzz to remove. In our culture it is respectful to our husbands to have it all waxed off." Deniz informed me.

We left the car and walked into the salon. Overhead bells tinkled as we went through a beaded open door and stepped into a buzzy, packed salon. That morning the temperatures outside were a humid thirty-five degrees and it was even steamier inside with no air con, just a few open windows.

"Hoşgeldiniz, welcome." An older lady in traditional ensemble sat next to a heavy, old-fashioned money box. She greeted and fondly kissed Deniz on each cheek. "I see you have brought your friend," she turned to me and shook my hand. "I am happy to meet you, my name is Nazla, I am Burcu's mother. Please take a seat."

Around the small room were women of all ages dressed in both European and Turkish-style clothes. Everyone was waiting to have their treatments as they sat on hard, orange, plastic seats.

To their left was a closed floral curtain and on the other side of the room was the hair-salon area with some washbasins and a wall-to-wall mirror. A few young girls squatted on low stools over customers' feet or hands as they worked meticulously giving pedicures or manicures. I could spy some customers sitting with their eyes closed, blown-up pink hoods covering their heads with accordion pleated hoses that stuck out—all attached to some kind of wire that eventually plugged into a socket behind them on the wall.

I was thrown back in time—sitting in a cinema watching a black-and-white Pathé News from the fifties. The scene reminds me of how my mother and grandmother would have their weekly shampoo and set, bouffant style, back in Ireland in a similar hair salon.

There was a swish of the floral curtain and a pretty lady with dark henna hair and rosy cheeks appeared, behind her a stunned-looking, pale-faced, teenage customer. The flushed lady moved towards me, her hand extended, "Ah, you must be Miriam, we have been waiting for you. Welcome to my salon, my name is Burcu, you have met my mother Nazla. I am honoured, you are my first yabanci customer". She beams. Let's get you a glass of Turkish tea."

"Aren't you the lucky girl!" Deniz piped up. "She is looking forward to having her first, Turkish wax, aren't you Miriam?" she tells Burcu. I remain silent.

"If you call yourself a friend of mine you cannot walk around with hairy legs. Now you are half-Turkish–half-Irish you must have this wax done..."

I had known Deniz from my original trip to

Turkey three years before. She was my first Turkish friend, we connected and knew each other's Irish/Turkish humour. Reluctantly I said, "OK, I trust you but I shall wait until later before I say the big thank you."

As soon as the word 'wax' was mentioned, quick as a flash Burcu called to a junior, "Please bring the wax pot to the centre of the floor."

The girl appeared with a big lump of congealed wax and placed it in a steel pot sitting on a lit Primus stove. Like a naïve tourist I sat sipping my tea, listening to the chatter and the click-clacking of knitting needles. I smiled at the women around me, they smiled back, the sisterhood united in our efforts to be beautiful and smooth of skin. With much activity the atmosphere still remained laid back and easy, Deniz joined in with the other friendly women to have her Turkish coffee cup read by the excited Nazla. As the wax started to bubble the young girl reappeared with a knife and placed it in the pot to sterilise it.

Burcu was still beaming by the curtain, "Miriam, come, take off your skirt and stand up on the bed in front of you. Hold on to the wall with your back to me."

Reading my expression of apprehension Deniz squeezed my hand, "Miriam go to it my brave wax warrior." I went along with her cajoling and assurances and followed Burcu. I was poised and in place for my wax when Burcu wheeled in the pot of molten, honey-coloured liquid. Pulling out the knife from the pot she smeared the hot, gooey wax onto my left leg—starting at my ankle then working her way up to my knee.

With a great effort to be calm I said through gritted teeth, "Burcu, the temperature of the knife is burning my skin, it is unbearable. Can you please cool the knife or the liquid, or do you have a long wooden spatula to spread a small amount of wax at a time?" She smiled at me, ignored my request or it was not understood, and completely wrapped the poor burning leg in strips of white cotton material. She patted it from top to bottom. Then, with an almighty swipe she tore the whole of the sheeting off my leg. I yelped like a helpless puppy, "Whoa!" I screamed—not caring who heard me. "Burcu, boy that hurts."

I looked over my shoulder, shocked. "For God's sake Deniz say something to your friend here. My leg looks like a freshly-plucked chicken's leg, it is red and raw."

From the other side of the curtain I heard giggles, then Deniz's voice of encouragement, "Come on, you can't stop now?" I took an extra-deep breath and succumbed to the same torture on the right leg.

As Burcu tore off the sheeting I screamed out, "That's it, no more, stop!"

She looked up in surprise, "What about your bikini line and under your arms?"

'Have you no mercy?' I thought. Shakily I turned around on the bed and looked down to see blistered burn marks on both legs.

"Deniz!" I yelled, "Get me out of here." With tears in my eyes I eased myself off the bed. Burcu continued to be puzzled by this deranged foreigner and she still held the hot knife in her hand... I pulled on my skirt then pulled back the curtain to a full audience of shocked eyes which stared straight at me, including Deniz'.

Burcu took my arm, "I am sorry this waxing has hurt you, but this is the traditional way." I thanked her, but at that moment I felt as if my whole body was on fire. I wanted to crawl away. I needed to have a coffee with something strong in it so I could calm my nerves which were shot to pieces.

Nazla would not take any money, "How can I take money from Deniz's friend when it is her first time to have waxing done in this way? Please stay." She called to the young girl "Please make some fresh, medium Turkish Coffee for our yabanci friend. Let me read the grains from your empty coffee cup, I have a good feeling about you living here."

In truth I do not enjoy the gritty taste or aftertaste of Turkish coffee and believe you me I have tried many strengths and qualities of the dark stuff. Apologising, "I am due to go to another appointment, please excuse me until another day." (It was a white lie, but I was desperate to get out of there.)

With great effort, Nazla heaved herself up to hug me. "It will get easier, come again soon." She looked at me with hope.

Deniz spoke to the women, "This is my friend's first waxing in our Turkish way, she has been brave."

The women cried out "Cesur, cesur*," as they tapped their spoons on their çay glasses and coffee cups. I blushed, embarrassed.

Deniz linked arms on the way out. "What are a few scars in the name of beauty?"

"I will tell you about scars, this trauma has brought back sad memories of the first time I went through similar pain. I was twenty-one, just arrived in London with only a suitcase and a lot of hope. I was preparing for an interview to be a croupier at the Playboy Club. Don't laugh, but the uniform was a bunny outfit and, yes, that meant wearing a white, fluffy ball stuck on to my derrière. A few days before the big interview my flatmate insisted on waxing my legs. Agony did not describe it."

"And did you get the job?" Deniz asked.

"No, on my way to the interview I fell down the stairs at Oxford Circus Underground Station, I was wearing the highest of red slingbacks. I twisted my ankle and got carted off to A&E. I never found out if I could have made it as a croupier."

"What job did you end up doing?" Deniz asked.

"Trainee Management with the John Lewis Group in handbags and gloves, dahling. I wore a uniform of black and white with thick tights, nobody was remotely interested in my legs, hairy or otherwise. From now on I am sticking to my Western way. When they need doing I will decide how and where to go. And if you don't mind Deniz, no more wax surprises please..."

"Miriam you need to learn that here in Turkey no matter how clever you may be if you have hairy legs you will not get that job.

To make it up to you, come and join my friends and I for lunch." Deniz pleaded.

"Deniz I would happily join you but, as I was getting ready for my surprise earlier today, I did not know you were planning to get me stretched out like a scorched hen." We laughed hysterically and hugged, still friends.

"Right now I feel battered, I just want to let my body drop into the salty sea water and allow these burning legs to cool off."

And so I was driven home by the dangerous Deniz.

When we arrived the car filled with a deafening drone of drilling, the air was thick with dust and Serjan was barking orders.

"What are your neighbours trying to do with their house?" she asked, shocked by the rubble bubble of mess and noise.

"Oh Deniz, don't ask or I shall have a mega rant. It is *Nightmare on Beach Haven*... Honestly... Serjan has decided he wants to be king of all that he views from his land and upgrade his home, copying some of the modern styling from ours. He has brought a team of workers with him and the noise and dust is endless—day and night. He is a man obsessed, and the sad thing is Neglin goes along with whatever he wants for a quiet life."

I could feel myself getting angry and upset. It was time to let my legs cool off and rest from the morning's waxing events.

We said our goodbyes. "Be firm and strong with this bully," were Deniz's parting words.

Later that evening I was grateful when CJ arrived home. We discussed the ongoing situation of Serjan who at this stage did not care who he upset or what he did to make his home a showpiece for all to see and be envious of.

"I came here for a reason CJ, wishing for peaceful restoring days. This is not my idea of a beach haven. CJ, are we naïve foreigners thinking we can fit in?

"Perhaps it has come down to moving, lock, stock and barrel again..." My words betrayed my drained emotions.

"Well, as it happens M, on my flight from Istanbul I met a man called Henry who lives in a traditional village a twenty-minute drive from here. He was sad to hear of what is happening and has suggested we visit as soon as we are able.

"What do you say if I go visit him and check out this area over the next weeks?"

"Just now Serjan is like a time bomb ready to go off at any moment, who knows what he will do next? Let's do it," I reply.

It was agreed that one morning CJ would seek out Henry's house in the peaceful village he recommended.

Meanwhile, still on the waxing trail some weeks later, I ventured alone into the world of waxing again—to another highly recommended salon. The owner's name was Zerrin. Having been relieved to have survived this bout of leg waxing without cause to roar or cry, Zerrin disappeared... only to reappear wielding a hot-wax-covered wooden spatula. "Miriam, it's time for you to have a Brazilian, it won't take long."

'Are you kidding? With the mental and physical scars of my past experiences, never, ever will I consider having a Brazilian, thank you very much.' I said this quietly to myself.

"Thank you for your kind offer, Zerrin, but that area does not wish to be waxed. Ever."

"OK, so let's try the ball of sugar with lemon on your bikini line," she urged me. Back she came smiling as she rolled this lethal ball in her hands. It looked like plasticine. "Don't worry Miriam, it's no problem," Zerrin assured me. Again I allowed myself to be persuaded, like a lamb to the slaughter.

Once she completed this torturous treatment I summed it up, "Zerrin I feel as if I have been skinned alive." She shrugged her shoulders, not understanding my reaction.

And still I went back for more punishment.

On another visit, Zerrin introduced me to a young girl. "Miriam this is my new assistant, Cihan. Would you mind if she does your waxing today?"

"Only if she can do it the European way," I replied.

"Of course, Cihan knows exactly what to do. I have trained her in your Western ways," she assured me. Naïvely, I went behind the canvas and wooden screen.

I hopped onto the bed then closed my eyes. I was thinking relaxing thoughts when Cihan called out, "Flex, flex your toes." She pushed, pulled and kneaded my skinny legs. I felt every swipe of the cotton as she removed the wax. Perspiration rolled off my flushed face and arms. I opened my eyes and looked down, only to see my bikini line smeared with oozy wax, long strips of cotton placed on top. With a powerhouse of strength Cihan grabbed the strips with her hands and tore them off my poor tender skin.

With an almighty roar, "Jee...zus H. Christ, for the love of God! Cihan, what are you doing down there?" The sticky wax was clinging to every orifice around the afflicted area, some of it adhered to the papery thin cover on the bed. With only half of my wax complete, "No!" I said. "That's it, no more waxing."

I scrambled and fumbled to get dressed while Cihan looked upset and confused at my outburst.

I pushed back the wooden screen with such force it fell over. I tripped and picked myself up, immersed in folds of paper. Threads of wax appeared like spun sugar sticking to my hands and they spread like a spider's web across my legs and bare feet. I looked in the mirror opposite: a ruddy face with damp hair. My clothes were saturated and clung to my pink skin. The adorable puppy in the Andrex advert runs along as the roll of toilet paper unfurls behind it. The reality for this mature woman was definitely not having quite the same cute impact. Globules of wax were glued to the sides of both legs and held them together. Some of the stuff sticking to my derrière scrunched up my now-creased, soggy skirt in a most unladylike fashion. I tried to separate my legs as I walked and wished to leave the salon with some sense of dignity, but the paper bedcover continued to tear into shreds as I moved forward.

I faced the firing line of Turkish women sniggering behind their magazines at this silly tearful yabanci.

I shouted across the room at Zerrin. "Never again Zerrin, do you hear me? Never, ever again am I going through this."

Three days later I was still cutting off the remains of the clinging, almost plastic-like wax from odd places, my legs more pliable as I walked more freely again. Not a pretty sight.

Since those first heady, searingly-painful close shaves I have to my great relief found two European-style beauticians who hail from Istanbul. They complete an almost Western-style waxing treatment. My advice—trust me on this—if you are in any way squeamish or have sensitive skin, take a major rain check. And remember, if you step into a small hair salon in a small town in Turkey, Eastern waxing is not for the faint hearted. If you see the scalding pots and knives, back-pedal, turn and quickly walk away. You have been warned!

Finding our
Piece of Paradise

Early one morning, unbeknown to me, CJ set off to drive to the village Henry lived in.

On the way CJ got lost. Thanks to meeting a young village boy who gave him directions CJ did not go to Henry's house but drove to a boutique hotel called *Cennet** some two-thousand feet up the mountain.

CJ returned home elated, "I have been on a bit of an adventure thanks to Henry's original invite. I have found a magical village and, nestled into the top of this mountain, is a small hotel. It is the kind of setting we have dreamed about living in. I am taking you away for a mindless recharge break—a million miles from the noise we have to endure here each day. Pack your bags, this time tomorrow we will be surrounded by silence."

I could literally hear that silence as I stepped out of our car that first evening.

The friendly owner appeared with a rotund roly-poly dog at his side. He introduced himself, "My name is Ozzie, CJ has explained where you have come from." He shook his head and picked up our cases. He escorted us down some rocky, sloping steps to a terracotta-coloured stone cottage. It was set on a plateau—its shimmering, thick, green-glass doors reflected incredible views of an almost biblical landscape that stretched for miles before and behind us. "Welcome to this mountain. Relax, be in the peace and quiet, nobody will bother you. We are here to take care of you so please ask for what you need. If you wish to join us I shall be serving wine on the upper terrace as the sun sets."

"Now that is something I never tire of," I replied. He shook our hands, turned and walked back up the steep steps with the dog at his heels.

That night I slept a drugged sleep and the long days followed with rest on the terraces. I swam in the icy, stone pool with water that came from the restorative healing streams further up the mountain. I gazed in disbelief at my spectacular environment. Slowly the events back at our house by the sea seemed distant and I removed from them.

Ozzie and I struck up a friendship. Each evening, all three of us sat together over dinner as the sun set and the moon and stars appeared. These were the magical, healing surroundings I had hoped to find when we arrived a year before.

CJ surprised me by extending our stay by five days.

We asked Ozzie, "What are the chances of us finding a small house here?"

"There are not many to choose from, perhaps four in total. Don't be shocked when you see them, as they are no more than open, four-legged concrete structures. One of the buildings is located below the hotel and the cottage you are staying in. It is a private space with no neighbours, just pine trees and birdsong." Ozzie seemed kind with a desire to help us.

"If you wish I can speak to the people who own the land. Then I can take you to view the houses," he offered.

I was not particularly interested in viewing properties. I was happy to let the menfolk do their research and report back.

Then curiosity got the better of me and one morning I walked down the rough shingle pathway that led from the hotel to a narrow country road.

Eventually it led me up to a track. As I walked along the stony terrain I was mesmerised by the striking scenery. Before me was the shell of a would-be-could-be house. Pale-pink marble steps led to a black, wrought-iron balcony of more marble and a front door of pine led into the main house. I stood for a while—looking out to a wild environment where, for hundreds of years, umbrella-topped pine trees had stood, proud and elegant.

I looked out to the green-and-yellow sunshine valley asking myself, 'Can I live in such isolation up this high mountain, away from people and my beloved sea?'

I made the same trip back to the concrete structure over the next few mornings. Each time I walked to the could-be house, with the warm healing sun on my face, I felt a great oneness in this natural environment. I listened to the birdsong and the sound of the cool breeze running through the magnificent, tall, protective pine trees that surrounded the property. I watched butterfly couples lightly flutter from plant to tree in unison. This was the real Turkey, the one to help me recover and manage my life again.

Now that we had found why we came to this part of Turkey my heart and body did not wish to go back and live next to Serjan and Neglin's house.

CJ and I discussed the possibility of moving to this piece of paradise. "What do you say M? We could put the beach house on the market as soon as we return. I already have a few people who are interested."

Again, we spoke to Ozzie who hailed from Istanbul. He had lived at his hotel for over ten years. "Miriam it has been the best decision I have ever made. In my old life I was a typical city man, a mad, city dweller known for rushing and pushing everyone around me. I was loud, rude and sometimes aggressive—living here has changed me forever. I am more mellow, more at peace and have no need to live in a city again. I love my life and count myself blessed to have found this land to build my hotel on. Life is good here, I am free.

My neighbours are gentle, kind people who only wish to give—as you will find out if you decide to come and join us."

Now keener than ever, we eagerly asked Ozzie over dinner, "What are the chances of taking on the house underneath us?"

"I believe the owners would be more than happy to discuss the possibility of you living here. You would be the first foreigners in this part of the village." Ozzie seemed keen too. He promised to speak to the people who owned the land.

Feeling more relaxed it was then time for us to return to the beach house. A light of possibility seemed to glow. It was time to face the demon and move our lives forward.

On returning to ours we lay in bed, with little chance of sleep due to the ever-growing building site and the even brighter lights (as on a football pitch) that illuminated our bedroom. We got up, got dressed and made our way to Serjan's house.

"Oh you are back, we thought you had gone away..." he sneered at us, his shiny, red-dyed hair and moustache catching the light. Neglin remained silent in the shadows of her terrace.

"Please Serjan, we are pleading with you to stop

the noise at this crazy hour of the night. Let us sleep and give us some peace."

He laughed in our faces, turned to walk away, then lunged at CJ with threats of how he could not bear to see us live in this Turkish community. "Why did you have to change your house and garden, why are you trying to be better than everyone else?" He spat the words out.

Neglin came running out trying to pacify him. "Serjan, stop this now! There is no need to be so aggressive or disrespectful to our good neighbours." But it was all to no avail.

We were appalled and shocked that someone could behave in this manner. It was the straw that broke the camel's back, our final sign. It really was time to move.

Back in the safety of our house, still reeling, I made a calming camomile tea while CJ nursed a large glass of brandy.

"I believe the plans for our move to the mountains will go ahead. I will do everything I can to ensure our new home in the village is completed by the time you return from the U.K." CJ spoke in a determined, firm voice I had not heard before.

When discussions were finalised and contracts were signed we set about making a plan to redevelop and redesign the new house to meet our basic needs.

When we first moved to Turkey the original plan was to spend three or four months there then return to the UK for about six weeks for the treatments I had found effective. With some relief it was time for me to head to Blighty.

How CJ completed this project I will never know. What I do know is that we were somehow led to this piece of paradise, this healing retreat.

After six weeks I returned excitedly to Turkey and CJ collected me from the Airport. With fresh faith and hope we drove up the mountain to the traditional Turkish village we were about to call home. A new chapter of this Turkish life-path was about to unfold.

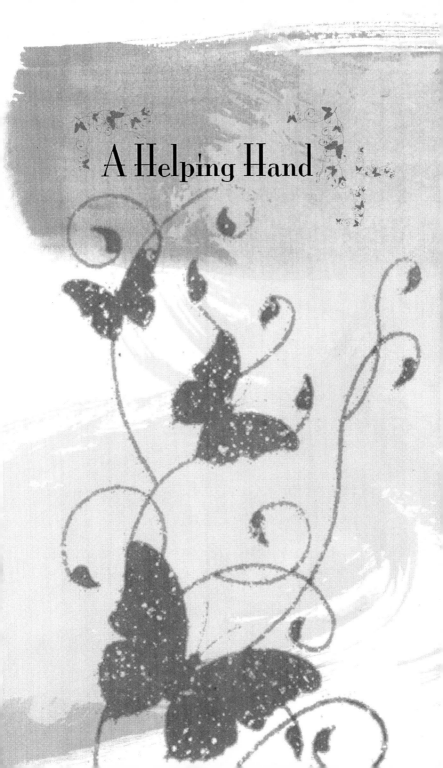

A Helping Hand

A doorbell rang, the pitch so high it startled me out of a deep sleep. Then came the sound of a cockerel with his cock-a-doodle-doo accompanied by some wild primate noises from down the valley. I was later informed they were two braying donkeys.

"Come on Miriam, rise and shine! It's your first morning in our new home, time to embrace the day." I heard CJ talking with far too much enthusiasm. He carried on talking but it might as well have been a foreign language, nothing registered in my mushy brain. I did not want to open my tired eyes. "Here is your dressing gown. I see you turning into a more traditional woman now that you are in this small village." He laughed as he draped the fabric on the bed. "Get up, get up, your new lady is here to help you, she is waiting outside."

"Where am I and what is that ringing sound?" I called out, but he was gone. Eventually I opened my eyes and looked around the bare room, we didn't yet have curtains on the open windows. Outside I spied a forest rising into the mountain, stretching up to a blue sky. I saw how CJ had fastened my most precious crystal ball (a gift from him many years before) to the centre of the curtain rails. Shimmering light flooded onto my bed and into the room. Moving rainbow colours splashed on to the white walls. Feeling the heat on this early morning, I wearily rolled over and pulled myself up onto the side of the bed. I reached for my watch from a little wooden makeshift table. I was two hours ahead of UK time. I realised why my energy was sapped, I had travelled for more than twelve hours from the UK to Turkey before CJ collected me late the night before. With anticipation he had whisked me back to our new home in a Turkish village, up a mountain.

It was time to face my first day at *Pink Pines*.

Wrapping myself tightly in my light cotton dressing gown I went from the bedroom to the bathroom, to splash my face and clean my teeth. How strange, 'Why is there a washbasin with a mirror outside the bathroom and then another one in the bathroom?' I saw my reflection, not a pretty sight at that hour, my complexion pallid, my hair standing up skew-whiff. This was not the time to get precious about how I looked, or the details of the layout of the house. I stumbled through to the lounge and moved to the front door in my bare feet.

Standing patiently on the sunny balcony was 'a slip of a girl,' as we say in Ireland. She stood, exuding an aura of calm. She was dressed from head to toe in shades of blue, yellow and lime green—coordination of colour, there was none. Every pattern and fabric clashed as if from a psychedelic time machine.

"Merhaba Miriam, hoşgeldiniz. I am Selma and I am here to help you." She stepped forward shyly and, with braceleted Turkish-style outstretched hand, pushed a bunch of creamy flowering thyme (encased in pink, sweet-smelling roses), into mine. "These are from my garden; soon we will grow many flowers in yours too." I looked down at the dusty scrubland. The only signs of life were deeply-lined tree trunks: tall, bendy olive trees that could tell many stories of life in the village and which had been there long before Selma or the house.

I was touched "Ah, so you are the lady I have heard much about. Thank you Selma and a warm welcome to my world that may feel a little foreign to you right now."

There was an innocent air about this young girl, her head covered in an ornately designed cotton headscarf which was trimmed with circles of white lace that framed her pretty round face and smooth olive skin. It covered most of her jet-black, luxuriant, shiny hair. Her dark-brown eyes were kind and smiling, somehow this mishmash of colours suited her. She was barefoot too.

She picked up a steel tray with a pot of steaming hot yaprak dolmasi,* a plate of gözleme* and some eggs. She must have been up since the crack of dawn cooking these favourite Turkish delicacies, such thoughtfulness.

"I will prepare breakfast. Don't worry, I know what to do," she smiled, wanting to please. "I have a husband and two children. I cook and keep house, I tend my garden each day."

She walked through the front door; I followed her as she headed to the kitchen. We had only a kettle, a Turkish teapot, a few tea glasses and some Turkish tea from the Black Sea in northern Turkey. I knew about quality tea thanks to my dear Turkish Deniz, who advised me on what tea to buy when I had first arrived at our beach haven a year before.

CJ had left fresh fruit. Selma skilfully cut it up and laid out her food offerings presenting it all on a plastic fold-up table which came complete with two plastic chairs.

Then she began the Turkish tea-making ceremony.

"Miriam we believe that a day without Turkish tea is like a day without sunshine. Our Turkish-tea ritual is an important part of our social culture. The Turkish teapot consists of one small teapot sitting on top of a larger one."

I made Turkish Tea each day at our beach house but Selma was preparing it in a different way. I watched, intrigued, as she filled the larger pot with cold water then placed it on the stove with the small pot on top. Just before the water boiled she removed the small warmed pot, placed several teaspoons of tea in it, and replaced its lid. She put it on top of the larger pot, and when the large pot boiled she slowly added the hot water to the dry tea in the small pot until it was half-full. Then she covered it with its lid. She looked at me and smiled. "We must let the tea and water infuse for at least five minutes. Then you can eat breakfast."

While the tea is brewing, let me tell you how Selma came to us.

Ozzie (who helped us organise the initial house details), remarked one evening over dinner at his place, "Miriam you have to have help at your new house."

"I already have an excellent lady where we live by the beach but she cannot travel so far," I said, warily.

"Don't worry this lady lives down the track from here. I know the family well, they are good workers, I will speak with her husband and tell him exactly what you need. She is honest; you will be pleased to know she is not into village tittle-tattle. That said, she does not speak English nor has she worked with a Westerner before, but your Turkish is good. Now you have the chance to learn a lot more words especially with domestic duties. No problem, I think you will like her." Conversation over, we carried on eating under the starry night.

Ozzie never asked about my background, he assumed I was a woman who kept house. I realised, reluctantly, that in Eastern culture everything goes through the head (male) of the family. Later that night once more CJ confirmed, "Remember Miriam, I have worked out of the Far East for many years, this is the way things are done here—it will not affect your independence or how you wish to work the running of the house or the maintenance of the garden. You just have to accept the differences. How we think and do as Westerners has no meaning or relevance in this culture." He hugged me, knowing how anxious I was after the drama of that first year at our beach house. With a reassuring, "Once you adapt and accept your new way of working and communicating up this mountain, life will flow. All will be well, and if you do not like how this lady works we can find someone else."

Hmmm... time would tell on this one.

Now Selma was here wanting to work with and help me.

Back in the kitchen, after five-and-a-bit minutes, Selma poured the hot, steamy nectar into my tea glass until it was half-full then added some hot water. Selma said, "Afiyet olsun*".

The taste and flavour of the tea was refreshing and complemented my first village breakfast at ours. I ate slowly, savouring each tasty morsel. I already knew from working with my first housekeeper, Cihan, and my friend Deniz, that according to local custom she would not join me.

"Will I unpack your case so you can get dressed when you have eaten your breakfast?" she asked.

I nodded. Selma left me alone to eat and ponder

my day ahead with some semblance of focus.

After breakfast I wandered into the back room where wall-to-wall, ceiling-to-floor, pale wood wardrobes and cupboards almost filled the space. Again, a room with a view of the forest. I christened it the dressing room. I found a linen summer dress hanging up, stuck it on, rubbed some cream on my dry face and embellished my lips with some bright lipstick.

I was about to go outside to view my surroundings when I heard the creaky sound of an ancient truck chug-chugging as it reversed up the dirt track... the driver pressing too hard on the accelerator. Following the truck were two men dressed in work clothes with caps to shield them from the sun. What a surprise to see CJ with Cihan, standing up in the back of the truck holding on for dear life to some old rope to keep them steady.

"Merhaba, here we are at last," CJ announced as the timid Cihan waved and smiled a sad smile. They had travelled thirty-five kilometres on the back of this open truck packed with the contents of our former home. Brakes screeched as the battered lorry finally made it to the top of the stony drive. I walked down the pink marble steps with Selma following at my heels. The cargo was swaddled in thick blankets and hessian tied up with knots of strong rope. This was the Turkish equivalent of a furniture removal company. CJ jumped down and helped Cihan do the same.

The driver called out "I am Kemal, this is my truck, my business, and I am here to help you unload," he proudly announced. His oversized frame struggled to remove itself from the sticky plastic beading of the seat of his truck. Eventually he managed to slide out and he walked around and undid the back of the crammed vehicle.

We introduced each other, to each other, and shook hands. With a nod of the head the men pulled on their caps. It was my first time meeting Ahmet, Selma's husband, and his kind neighbour who had come along to help as well. His name was Ali. What a new homecoming.

Ahmet was a man of more senior years to Selma's youthful looks, his working life outside clearly showed on his tanned face. His eyes shone, he was warm, friendly and quiet, only speaking when necessary. Initially Selma and Cihan were reluctant to talk and interact with each other.

Selma called out, "I will make some fresh çay." But the group agreed to unload the truck first and have tea later.

This shy girl spoke to the men, "I think it is better for you, as you are stronger, to lift out the heavy furnishings first and carry them up to each room. Then we can form a line from the truck to pass each box and carry them into the house. Miriam and CJ, if you agree, let's start." Selma had obviously made a plan prior to the arrival of the truck.

Impressed, this was one strong lady. "Selma and I are going to get along just fine, thank you Ozzie!" I spoke to CJ in hushed tones.

CJ called out, "Be sure to lift and carry everything in with care so our belongings remain undamaged."

Kemal led the men with brisk efficiency.

Cihan and Selma, silently, relentlessly worked together as they moved around the house, gliding from room to room. There was no rush, they maintained an even, slow pace where each box or item was carefully placed in the appropriate room. Then CJ and I unpacked.

For a man of such proportions even Kemal was of a delicate touch and step. Drinking a glass of water he eventually drove off with an exchange of lira and a handshake for a job well done.

Now feeling more at ease with each other, Selma and Cihan disappeared into the kitchen. I could hear their chatter exchanging information about their families and backgrounds. They reappeared, "We have prepared salad with hard cheese from my goats," proclaimed a proud Cihan, "Miriam and CJ come, come, you must eat." They spoke together.

We went into the kitchen to sit awhile and fuel ourselves.

Cihan and Selma sat together cross-legged on cushions upon the lounge's wooden floor. They shared their food from one plate whilst they concentrated on unpacking boxes and various items wrapped up in layers of newspaper.

"Why," I exclaimed to CJ, "look our valuable Collesseum Wedgewood dinner service with our much-used teapot—the one with the narrow curved spout—is all in one piece." Hurrah. It was a cherished wedding gift from our respective families. I breathed a sigh of relief.

Many hours later CJ stood by the front door, "Are you ready Cihan? It is time to say goodbye. I will drive you back to your home."

"Hold on," I said, "you came in the truck. Where is your car?"

"Darling, do you think I am crazy, that I would stand up with these bones in that antiquated lorry to be thrown about for thirty five kilometres? I parked at the bottom of the track and boarded the truck for the last run up the hill. "OK, so I was trying to impress you as your superhero!"

Selma laughed and called him Superman, minus his red cloak.

I walked over to Cihan. There were no hugs, she formally shook my hand, her eyes brimming with tears.

"Thank you for the last eighteen months Cihan, for teaching me the first threads of my new life in this part of the world. I am truly grateful for your tireless help. Please accept these gifts for you and your family. May you continue to have a good working life wherever you work." I gave my little speech in my best Turkish. Loyal Cihan took the package but could not reply.

CJ interrupted, "Miriam, is this going to be the long Irish goodbye? We are all feeling emotional, let's go Cihan."

In her new role Selma went to the fragile Cihan, gave her a big hug, and kissed her on each cheek as she wiped her tears away. Then she was out the door, gone with one last wave as she walked slowly, head bowed, with CJ down the track. I would probably never see her again.

Selma left too, with a promise to return the next day.

The house was starting to feel like home. My brain was in overload and in need of some rest. I fell into bed for a few hours of slumber to recharge.

The following morning I awoke apprehensively, waiting for the intrusive sounds to envelop my morning... The banging, the hammering, the drilling and the months of shouting by Serjan were replaced with an uplifting chorus of birdsong which claimed the day, even the braying of the two vulgar donkeys was reassuring.

CJ turned to me "How does it feel my little beach babe now that you are about to become the *Walking Irish Woman of the Silent Mountains*?"

"I'll let you know; give me six months," I replied.

Then it was time to enjoy a relaxing breakfast on the top terrace. We absorbed the magical landscape of pine trees, the sweep across the green valley where sunlight reflected on the trees in front of us. Selma, true to her word, arrived with a pickaxe, a shovel on her shoulder and a plastic bag filled with leafy plants. Her skirts were tucked into an elastic waistband of what I can only describe as pyjama bottoms.

"Günaydın, Merhaba I am going to prepare your garden. It may take time to dig this terrain. As you can see it is hard and dusty now and when our winter arrives it will be soft and muddy."

"But Selma, surely it is too hot to work this dry and rocky land at this time of the year?"

"It is no problem for me." Within minutes she was on her hands and knees digging, hacking the earth for all she was worth, oblivious to anything else. Brave lady. After her first hour's work, with beads of perspiration running down her face, she called to me, "Miriam, look at this rich, nutritious, black soil. By our second spring (November) you will have healthy plants, next year maybe you will have fruit growing on this old plum tree."

She shook the small leaves of the shady tree above her.

What did I know? I would trust her wisdom on such matters. Then the hoeing and weeding began.

"Selma, please come and sit in the shade, have a refreshing çay."

"Thank you, I must keep working until this is finished. Now I will do some planting." She worked on without a break but accepted a bottle of cool water which she guzzled in one long glug. She repotted some rather tall and prickly cacti into larger pots. Aloes and yuccas we had transported from the beach house also went into the fresh, cool, dark earth.

Through Selma I was learning how the women in these villages undertake work that we would never imagine doing in the West. My claim to fame with gardens thus far had been the ability to grow herbs and rocket in pots or to voice my ideas for the garden while CJ implemented them to great success back in Blighty. But to actually get down and dirty and work in that heat and humidity was beyond me. As the day passed my respect for, and appreciation of, Selma grew.

At noon the blistering sun hung above Selma's kneeling body. CJ and I walked around our new home discussing how we would make the garden user-friendly and easy to maintain. We also wanted to create restful areas under the shade of the olive trees.

"What about building another terrace below this one? We can lie or sit with views out to the wildness of the forest and hills beyond. Perhaps we can have a long, bricked seating area with cushions. I have seen this done in many Turkish gardens," I suggested.

CJ responded, "Clever M—being able to lie down and listen to the silence in the shade, with views we could only dream about in our past life. Let's draw it out first then we will speak to Selma. She can ask Ahmet if it is possible. Maybe he will be happy to do the work with his skilled building friends."

I was distracted by huffing and puffing sounds to my right and initially thought Selma had been overcome by the searing heat after her high-energy workload of the morning. But no, coming up the track was an elderly villager dressed in long floral pyjamas and a loose-fitting top, her hair covered in what could have been some white sheeting. Out of breath she bustled towards us, her generously proportioned body moving from side to side.

On seeing the figure Selma jumped up and went over to help the woman. "Merhaba," she called out to us, her face glowing. Selma fetched a chair and placed it under the shade of the plum tree. She poured her a glass of water. The woman sat down gratefully, a jumbo hessian bag stuck out from under her arm. Perspiration rolled down her face. Her white scarf and her top were stained with moisture.

"This is Ahmet's mother, Ebru, who lives further down the track from my house." Selma introduced us. She seemed a friendly soul.

Animated though still out of breath Ebru spoke, "I arrived at dawn after forty-five days away on the trip of my life to Mecca."

She pulled open the hessian bag eagerly and presented us with a large packet of sweet medjool dates from the Holy City. I thanked her with a bow. I spied the head of a toy camel peeking out.

Ebru pulled the camel from the bag. She pressed some buttons, placed it on the ground, and the thing came to life with flashing red eyes. With a loud, completely out-of-tune rendition of the call to prayer, Ebru announced, "I wish to welcome you to your new home and a peaceful life in our village. I have lived here for over fifty years."

In the Muslim religion the Muezzin summons the people to pray five times a day in melodic tones (unlike the flashing camel).

CJ, myself, Selma and Ebru sat in a circle in the heat laughing, until finally the camel was quiet again. We thanked Ahmet's mother for her kind words and her gifts. It was time for each of us to cool off and to eat a little. Later CJ and I would admire Selma's outstanding work, producing a patch of vibrant garden in a matter of hours.

Perhaps the camel was a sign all would be well at Pink Pines... the place where we could fit in and would finally call home.

I have since removed the batteries from said flashing, red-eyed toy. It remains hidden away... until Ebru's next visit.

Turnaround

Bliss... Saturday morning. I was roused by the gentle sound of wedding drums beating further up the mountain, the day spread out like a blank canvas, mine to do with as I wished. CJ was lost in the city of Izmir, a three-and-a-half hour drive from the village. "Don't worry, darling," he assured me as he left at the beginning of the week, "I'll be back within forty-eight hours." It was day five and still there was no sign of his return.

I took a shower. Feeling refreshed I stepped out of the bathroom, only to be interrupted by the sound of heavy drilling, or was it an impending earthquake? No, the metal toilet roll holder did not jangle. I marched across the lounge and looked out of the window. Crikey! A bright yellow JCB digger was on our stony track. The heavily moustached man behind the wheel was pulling levers, lifting great chunks of red soil and oversized boulders out of the rock face.

I phoned CJ. "Hi darling, there is a JCB on the drive making a bit of a racket. Any ideas?"

"Oh yes, good news. I forgot to mention that an area for the cars is being dug out so we can turn around and drive down the dirt track onto the narrow main road. The man promised to come last week."

Heaven forbid that he would give us prior notice or warning.

"Jeez CJ, the noise is deafening. I was hoping to eat breakfast in peace and quiet. This reminds me of my other life back at the beach house. I really thought that was a closed chapter?" I was feeling rattled.

"M, as you know, we must show gratefulness

when the workers appear. It's all part of the charm of living in Turkey, never knowing if the work will get done on the appointed day or not. This is just a small blip. Be patient and make sure he is offered çay, keep him sweet."

He was far too cheerful for this hour.

"Is there anything else I need to know...?"

"Not to my knowledge, darling." He tried to placate me.

"More importantly, when are you coming home?" I asked.

"Hmmm, not sure, will call you later and update you." CJ rang off.

Selma glided into the lounge, as each day passed she blossomed, growing in confidence. With a flurry of excitement, "Miriam I am so happy, Ahmet has bought me a shiny, new, sewing machine. I have made you a linen laundry bag, see, it ties up with sailor's rope." I laughed as she threw it over her shoulder to demonstrate how she would use it.

"I have seen how you like to drink your coffee hot. I have knitted you a coffee warmer for your coffee holder." It was a perfect fit for my steel pot. Yet again I was touched by her thoughtfulness.

The beat of the drums grew louder.

As Selma prepared breakfast I noticed that her hands were covered in a henna design, another sign of a pending wedding celebration.

She placed the fresh food on a tray and carried it outside to the sunny top terrace. The pounding noise resounded around me, it was impossible to eat. I walked back into the kitchen, tray in hand, and relaid the table. With my earplugs firmly in place I desperately tried to block out all the noise, the vibrating floor, even my body and brain were pulsating.

Breakfast over and earplugs removed, I heard men in loud voices underneath the lounge windows. I walked outside to the top terrace, to check what was amiss. A mixing and sloshing of fluid being moved around in a container caught my attention. Ahmet and his old friend Volkan (who lived some thirty-five kilometres away) were mixing water and white paint in a recycled yogurt bucket. They were slapping this watery liquid (a sort of whitewash emulsion paint) onto the dirty wall under the staircase.

Like a madwoman I ran down the stairs.

"Ahmet, Volkan, what are you doing? Who told you to do this work?" As my anger rose so did the pitch of my voice. "CJ did not mention anything about having the outside wall painted before he went to Izmir."

Feeling agitated, "Please can you move all the plants and garden furniture out of the way. Surely you have to brush and wash this dirty wall before any kind of painting can be done? What is this white stuff anyway?" I pointed to the grimy wall and the frothy liquid.

Clearly embarrassed, Volkan put his hands up to cover his face and looked the other way.

"Speak to Selma, speak with her," he said in muffled tones. "I cannot speak to you."

"What is this about?" I asked. My feminine feathers were becoming ever more ruffled.

"I will not be treated so disrespectfully, nor have I any wish to talk to the hand."

I stormed back up the stairs into the house to

find Selma.

"What is going on here?" I asked. "Why are the men painting under the stairs? Why can't the job be done properly, like moving the plants and furniture away from the wall, washing down the wall and why are they not using real paint? And why, oh why, is Volkan covering his face and refusing to answer my questions?"

Selma calmly took my hand and guided me to the kitchen.

Exasperated. "For heaven's sake Selma, what's Volkan's problem?"

"Miriam, please sit and let me make you a Turkish tea. I will explain the whys."

Once the tea was made and poured into çay glasses, Selma joined me.

"Volkan is only doing what is perfectly normal and natural in our culture. He wanted to help Ahmet as CJ said the outside of the house needed painting. They wanted to surprise him for his return."

"What about a discussion with me first and then making a plan?" I asked.

Selma, bless her patience, continued in reassuring tones. "In our culture, especially in these small villages, a man cannot talk to or look at another man's wife. It is disrespectful. Please do not be angry Miriam."

Eventually I calmed down and got over my hissy fit. I realised yet again how different our cultures were. This feisty Irish woman used to getting things done, never giving a single thought to who was male or female. Volkan, the poor man, no wonder he was shocked and embarrassed by my forceful and rude outburst.

"How would he know how to behave towards you?" Selma asked. She was right, he had been faced with a hysterical foreign woman, how could he understand why there was such drama? Equally, how daft of me to get so worked up about them painting a wall that wasn't how I wished it to be.

Selma went to speak with the men, acting as mediator between East and West. She explained to her husband and Volkan why I was upset. They nodded. To my relief they whitewashed only a triangle of wall under the marble stairs and left for the day, leaving a trail of white, speckled blobs on the terrace, on the plants, on the wooden garden chairs and on the table. Guess who would have to clean it up. Women's work, don't you know.

After four hours of incessant noise, finally the metal monster and its driver, high on copious glasses of çay, left as well—with a smile and a wave.

Relieved—the gift of silence enveloped me and I set out to walk up the mountain, breathing deeply the clean calming air. Once I reached the top I stopped to admire the stunning views sweeping across the valley towards the traditional Turkish beach of Inlice Bay. The sun was high in the sky. Feeling sticky and hot I made my way back down the mountain to the rejoicing beat of the swelling sound of the drums.

I passed a house alive with activity, where a makeshift outdoor kitchen was set up. Many hands, women's of course, were briskly working towards some significant village event. Mammoth preparations were in full swing. In the sweltering heat the women gave orders to their men as hundreds of white plastic tables and chairs were unloaded from a trailer attached to a tractor. A few men in open, dirty shirts half-heartedly worked to place an awning between sturdy trees. Many waved, "Merhaba. Come later. Join our feast. Come and dance and share this celebration with us. We are waiting for you."

The smell of cooking saturated the air as the women lit open fires and placed large steaming cooking pots, the size of oil drums, on top. An older, craggy-faced man was hunched over a dry grassy patch with a scythe in his shaky hand. He slowly hacked away in the overgrown field. Hopefully the chairs and tables would be lined up on more even ground later.

Surrounded by cables leading to large speakers, an overwhelmed teenager was given the job of testing the unpredictable sound system. With a creaky sound here and a strangulated booming noise there, it was not boding well. Amongst this buzzy activity three men in nomad-style clothes and head coverings got out of a white car and pulled out their musical instruments from the boot. "We would like to practise with the sound system switched on," I heard them call out to nobody in particular. Live Turkish music evokes great emotion and feelings, where one is drawn spellbound to dance and move—even for those whose feet and hands are less coordinated. The musicians stood in the centre of the cleared grassy area, strummed for a while, then played their magnetic ritual songs.

Men stood on rickety handmade ladders and chairs, shouting and singing out of tune, trying to keep in time with the beat of the drums and the music. They were hastily arranging some primitive lighting, illuminating the musicians in hopes of adding to the atmosphere for this party after dark. İnşallah*...

I walked back up my dirt track to the house. I spotted Selma opposite the new car area digging feverishly with a large pickaxe. She grabbed a spade, throwing red soil over her shoulder. She looked up, wiping the perspiration from her brow and face with her headscarf originally tied around her head like a bandana.

"Miriam, the digger man dumped rocks and soil on my young fig trees. I have to save them."

She looked exhausted. You have heard of digging for buried treasure... well this was a case of digging for buried fig trees, gold to the villagers, as every fig is precious.

The ever-dedicated Ebru, Ahmet's mother, she of the red-eyed camel fame, has a stall where she sells the village produce at the Sunday market, including fresh figs when they are in season. The unsold fresh figs are dried by her in the hot sun on the steps leading up the back of her unfinished house. Or as my girlfriend calls it *The Stairway to Heaven*. Ebru sits on a cushion on her concrete veranda, legs stretched out in front of her for hours at a time. She sometimes dusts the figs lightly in flour, hooks them through string making a circle, half a kilo at a time.

Back to Selma's predicament. "Selma, I am sorry about the buried trees. What was that man thinking this morning? I hope you retrieve them and the trees will continue to grow and yield fruit later in the season.

"By the way, what is this sudden busyness further up the mountain? Why even the men are working at full pace today."

"Oh, that is my neighbours' seventeen-year-old daughter's wedding reception." You must know the sound of beating drums means a wedding is about to take place nearby? Surely you received an invitation?" Selma asked. "No worries or stress here, there is little planning. Arrangements are made at the last minute. Out of respect for the elders of the village and the only yabanci, you will have a front row seat with the best view of the new bride and the evening's proceedings." As if I needed reassuring.

Eventually, I twigged. A few days previously two youthful girls had appeared on a beat-up motor bike. They jumped off the bike (it was unusual to see girls riding motorbikes in these parts) and ran up the pink marble steps to my house. The girls handed me a roll of newspaper tied up with a piece of lilac ribbon, an envelope attached. Excited, one of the twosome announced, "Merhaba, I am Gozda and this is my cousin Melek. Here is my wedding invitation. I am to be married in a few days."

"What an unexpected surprise, thank you." I smiled at this innocent-looking teen.

"In our village everyone who lives here is invited, no need to buy a new outfit for the reception, show up as you are and we will give you a thousand welcomes. Nobody is competing to wear expensive clothes or accessories." She gushed. "I shall be the princess for two whole days from the tips of my toes to the top of my head." She danced animatedly. "I am counting the hours. I dream of how my future husband will not be able to take his eyes off me as I sparkle and shimmer on our special day. He will hold our wedding celebration and me in his memory forever, and so will I."

Naïve Gozda took a deep breath then the tears started to flow. "I am also sad as my future husband lives forty kilometres away. I shall be leaving my family and this village to live with his parents and family," she lowered her head.

Her pretty cousin put an arm around her, "Don't worry we will come and visit you often." Gozda sighed; they watched and waited whilst I undid the ribbon around the newspaper. Out rolled a white and lilac towel and the invitation. It was a white card, typed very simply with the name of the bride and groom, the family names and the locations of both receptions over two days.

Why the present? I still have no idea but what a generous thought.

"Bring your husband, there will be lots of dancing, we are waiting for you!" Now smiling again Gozda blew me a kiss, jumped back onto the bike then they roared down the track, engine spitting, clouds of dust in their wake.

"Good luck in your new life." I called after them.

Back to that Saturday's blank canvas... it was filling in far too quickly for my liking. The drums continued their gentle beat whilst local villagers, family and friends began to arrive. The lively pitch of voices and laughter filled the air with what I now knew to be a wedding celebration. The rising smoke became thicker as more fires were lit.

My head was buzzing. It was time to head to sleep for a few hours, earplugs firmly in place.

It was nearly dark when I stirred to the sound of disco music and the flashing of lights. The chatter and banter of the guests, along with animated children's laughter, echoed around and down the valley. The wedding party was in full swing. The walls of my house were vibrating. I stood on the upper balcony to take in the ambience of my first village wedding. The smell of meat from the barbecue wafted upwards and towards the house (perhaps a goat or sheep was turning on a spit over hot coals for this special occasion). I could not see but I could feel this spellbinding atmosphere.

Below me, I saw the lights were switched on. There in the yellowy golden shadows, head down, arms outstretched in the traditional male pose, clearly oblivious to anyone, was CJ. He was dancing as only he can, his left foot not knowing what his right foot was doing, to the enthusiastic Turkish group as they gathered speed.

No longer lost in Izmir, but lost to the sound of the music. He looked up.

"Hello darling, I thought I would surprise you. How about a romantic dinner under the stars tonight?" I smiled as I went into the house to open a bottle of chilled white wine from the fridge. I grabbed two glasses and returned to join him. We stood on the lower terrace and raised our glasses to each other.

"To the happy wanderer who has finally decided to return," I said.

We gazed into the misty direction of the wedding party and chorused, "To the bride and groom—good fortune, may you have a long and happy life together made complete with healthy children in the fullness of time."

I lit some candles and hung some oil lanterns on the branches of the olive trees surrounding us. We enjoyed a dinner for two while soaking up the now heady mood of the wedding celebrations.

As we retired for the evening, the drums carried on a-beating with music playing until eleven o'clock sharp (as the law rules here). Two owls, hanging out on the edge of an old broken branch on the tall pine tree in front of the house, hooted, lulling us into a deep slumber.

Life at Pink Pines had turned around, my Saturday calmer and complete.

Dog Adopts Foreigners

(with a fouling fowl)

One cold and windy morning I was out walking on my own, however I sensed I was being followed. A clammy fear overtook my body, somewhat panicked I turned slowly and then looked down. There on my right was a stocky mongrel the size of a Labrador. Intense dark-brown eyes stared up at me, her tail wagging round and round like a propeller.

'Hi, remember me? Don't be frightened, I like humans; except those who ride bicycles or motor bikes. It's the other female dogs I am not so keen on. You can be my walking buddy if you like?' This roly-poly dog—a mix of goat, a bit of Basil Brush's tail and a foxy face, whose coat was a faded-hay colour—resembled a hairy tub of butter.

I realised we two had met before, at the Cennet boutique hotel a few hundred metres above us. When we arrived that first evening, having escaped from our chaotic beach home looking for respite and peace, a bouncy, stocky body greeted us with the same enthusiasm she showed that cold morning as we walked along the track together. I remembered how Ozzie, the owner of Cennet, named each room after dogs in his family. Our room was named after Martha, her name inscribed on a plaque which hung on the stone wall outside the glass door.

At Pink Pines, as we adapted to the mountains and village life, CJ brought up the subject of dogs time and time again. "M, you know since childhood there have been dogs in our family and what they mean to me."

"Yes, I know only too well how you feel about these four-legged animals you call friends, and I know where this conversation is going. Jeez, CJ, you also know how I feel about dogs. I don't mind when they are little balls of fluff but when they grow into sharp-toothed canines they give me the jitters," I spoke apprehensively.

My memory gates burst open, whisked me back to being that scared, little girl. Walking to school with my sisters each morning dogs seemed to sense my fear, sought me out to sink their teeth into my skinny little legs, Alsatians in particular. Even in adulthood terror swept over me like a hot sweat, moving diagonally across my body, every time I saw a dog approach.

"M, you could learn how to be around these loyal animals and in time lose this ingrained fear. I miss not having a dog or two around. What do you say we go find a puppy from the dog sanctuary?"

"Hmmm..." My guarded, unenthusiastic response. After much cajoling, I finally agreed. "OK, OK, let's go visit the local dog sanctuary. We'll take a look but I am not promising anything."

"Darling, I promise that your heart will melt when you see these dogs and how they need a loving home." CJ remained buoyant, hoping he could help change my mind.

After visiting the sanctuary my feelings for these innocents had softened, but I still left without a furry, four-legged friend. I did not have his yearning; much to his disappointment.

Back to that morning on the track... Martha, sensing my fears, carried on trailing me as if it was the most natural thing to do. I started to relax too as my new best friend walked with me up to Pink Pines. She was shivering and hungry. 'What do I feed her?' I asked myself.

I telephoned CJ. "I have a new walking buddy."

I announced.

"Oh, that's good, who? Selma?"

"No, it's that funny looking dog from Cennet. She has followed me back to the house. She's shivering and seems hungry. Do I feed her?"

"Well that's a turn up for the books; I can't wait to see this with my own eyes." He laughed.

"Put down some scraps of meat from the fridge on foil. You'll soon find out if she is hungry or not." I could sense he was thrilled at the prospect of a dog joining us. With trepidation I followed CJ's instructions and placed some cold köftes* at her feet. She ate the lot with a 'Please, I beg you, can I have some more?' She licked and licked the foil until it tore, giving a short sharp bark when I tried to remove it, scaring the living daylights out of me.

Selma arrived at the house as I poured water into a plastic bowl with the dog at my side. "Well, well, Miriam, so Martha has found you. Martha is the village dog. She appeared one day when Ozzie was building the Cennet Hotel. She was a tiny runt only a few weeks old, nobody knows where she came from. Over the years she has been passed from one family to another. She lives outside most of the time, barking her way through the night, rarely sleeping until the sun comes up. She is a lovable soul, probably nine years old. I believe she has come to you for a reason. She could have a good home if CJ and you want her to stay." Selma knelt down to stroke Martha.

When CJ came home that evening Martha bounded over to him as if they were long lost buddies. Martha sat at his feet enjoying the attention and affection. These two have been bonding ever since.

The following morning Martha was waiting outside the front door, instinctively knowing we were heading out to walk. She seemed happy to have our company and ran down the dirt track, stopping every so often and turning around, as if to say, 'Come on, keep up, I know the trail...' She made sure we were following. That evening, as the sun set, Martha sat on the top step.

"Come on darling, come inside, come into the warmth of our house." CJ tempted her in with a handful of dog biscuits. She took the bait, padding into the lounge. I found a cotton-fibre mat and placed it near the cosy, warm, wood-burning fire. She slept deeply that night, her body heaving in and out.

A few days later it appeared that Martha was going nowhere out of range of Pink Pines or CJ. "Perhaps we ought to buy her a proper doggie bed..." suggested CJ.

"Does this mean you want her to stay? Because it seems to me that Martha has already made the decision to adopt us in her dotage years." Did I want to be the damp blanket on CJ's yearning to have a dog? The answer—no.

Arriving home with a scrunchy, quilted bed for Martha; he placed it by the fire. We called Martha into the lounge. She followed behind CJ, spied the bed, jumped straight in and then rarely left it, with the exception of full moon nights.

We have no need for alarm clocks, Martha wakes us with a rise-and-shine morning bark. 'Come on guys, let's go walking.' As soon as she sees CJ and I putting on our trainers she bounces backwards and forwards, jumping at us to get a move on like a puppy, all waggy tailed. Tubby as she is she can happily walk for hours. There is a gushing stream on the route back to the house. Martha throws herself in and splashes around as she drinks from the crystal-clear, fast-moving water. 'Come on in guys, join me. This is so refreshing, my paws are loving this cool sensation.'

After walkies, more sips of water and a handful of biscuits she heads back down the dirt track to take up her regular occupation—red squirrel watch—and torments the little devils. She chases them, barking as she goes, thinking she can catch them, as they run up and down the pine trees. I have seen her attempt to climb the telegraph pole. Other mornings she sits at its base as if cast in stone, not moving a muscle. Sometimes exasperated she stands against the pole looking up with a vengeful, 'Don't even attempt to come down, if you do your name is 'Red' and you may not live to tell the tale of being a squirrel.'

The squirrels are far too clever for Ms. Rotund Martha. They sit on top of said telegraph pole smirking with a 'Catch-me-if-you-can' then they dart down to the overhanging trees by the wall. Like flashes of lightning they run across the track and chase each other up the pine trees again with a 'Ha ha... we have beaten you again missy.'

Stubborn Martha will not be beaten as she jumps at the wall barking or she runs full pelt down the valley baring her teeth with indignation at the victorious squirrels.

Through the euphoria of CJ's wish being granted by Martha adopting us he pushes the boundaries even further.

"Let's try and live off the land," he said one morning over breakfast, a faraway look in his eyes. "Not quite 'Me Tarzan, you Jane'—more New Age Eco-Man. Imagine the joy of rearing chickens, the excitement of collecting our own eggs each morning? Perhaps with Selma's help and advice we could keep a goat or a sheep. She could show us how to make yogurt."

Shortly after this a little miracle fell out of the sky, a ballet-trained, precise-stepping chick of pale-brown and darker feathers landed on our terrace.

"Where has this little beauty come from?" CJ asked animatedly. The young chicken moved amongst the foliage on the terrace leaving a runny mess in her wake.

Martha barked to show her disapproval and was heard to mutter, 'What the blo... hell, the last thing I need is a feathery critter taking over. I was here first...' She growled if the chicken came anywhere close. The confident chick was not put off by a mere dog, not even Martha. We christened her Matilda or Mattie.

A few mornings later, Selma revealed, "My friend Dilek, who lives further up the mountain, is missing a chicken from her flock. It fits the description of Matilda. For now it looks as if she wants to stay, we best feed her."

We thought it best for Dilek to collect Matilda so she could return to the bosom of her feathered family. But Dilek generously insisted we keep Matilda as a work-in-progress gift.

"She will yield you fresh eggs a few months down the line," Selma announced, smiling.

CJ, Mr Eco-Man, was as happy as a pig in... Yet

again another wish had been granted.

I was a city girl with a beach babe outlook on life (well, that's how I used to view myself through my rose-tinted glasses). I did not know the first thing about rearing or feeding a chicken, apart from the fact that they laid eggs.

Thanks to Selma Matilda thrived. "Feed her every morning and evening with either rice or wheat grains. It is ok for her to eat a diet of high carbs and low fat for now."

My biggest challenge was to stop Mattie doing naughties on the sunroof of my car. I discovered when the sun set she flew onto the roof, curled up and slept until sunrise.

I spoke with Selma's husband, Ahmet. "Is there any way you can build a coop with a good-sized run to keep Mattie away from my car? She must be safe from the foxes that roam at night and have a warm nesting area. Ahmet, you can imagine how CJ is counting the days to when Mattie starts to lay eggs." He promised to create one as soon as he was able.

CJ and Mattie have built up a lasting rapport as they cluck to each other all the time. Mattie loves it when CJ gives her a little tickle under the chin. I think this is taking being in touch and getting back to nature a little too far.

She can be a noisy soul, as soon as I appear on the upper terrace she makes a beeline for me with her high-pitched cluck, 'Where is my food?' Stubborn, like her four-legged enemy, Martha, Mattie flies onto my arm and presses her beak into my shoulder, 'I cannot live on worms alone. I need my grains of rice too.'

Martha continues to ignore Mattie. She has other things on her mind. Romantic she is not, but she seems to exert a magnetic attraction on some of the male dogs in the village. There is a queue to drink from her trough, or they cock their legs on my precious Jasmine plants while gazing up at her. With desire on their minds they are desperate to attract her attention. At a safe distance, draped across the pink marble steps in a teasing manner, she flirts with the boys then turns away as if they do not exist.

One male dog named Raki (after the traditional Turkish, milky-coloured, aniseed-tasting drink) has a longstanding dream. 'From the first time I saw you Martha, all those years ago, it was instant for me—there was chemistry. All I have wanted ever since is to get it on with you so we can live happily ever after.'

Raki is half her size, with a pale blonde, weathered coat and sticky out paws which are not in balance with the remainder of his long, low body. He appears randomly, hoping the element of surprise will trip Martha's curiosity.

'Martha, oh Martha, surely you must know how I feel? Even with your disdainful looks I carry the torch. One day you will change your mind and realise I am the one for you.' With that he swaggers over to another plant and cocks his leg, leaving his scent. Martha looks the other way, licking her paws as if that is the most important item on her agenda for that day. Dejected for now Raki leaves the area. Loyal and besotted with this great big lump he never gives up and continues to visit.

As time passed I agreed with CJ. "OK, I put

my hands up. Keeping a dog, especially the gentle natured Martha, is helping me lose my fear of dogs. Who would have thought it was possible? With her foibles and funny old ways, she managed to tune in to me from day one. By deciding to adopt us Martha has given me the confidence to enjoy her company."

While CJ managed to manifest his wishes we also found ourselves playing host to other animals and creatures who were not on our wish list.

It started with a gecko, 'Hey guys if you want a decent home with love and food... make your way to the pink house with the foreigners. Yeah, they seem to love us quirky, funny types. I mean, look at Martha putting roots down after all these years. She's got it sussed for her retirement. Let's go and find ourselves nirvana.' And one by one they took up residence at ours.

The first to arrive was little George, with his swishy, turquoise tail as he ambled around us on the lower terrace in the mornings in search of breakfast. When it was hot he headed to Martha's water, a large log with the centre cut out making two troughs. George jumps onto the log, slides into the water and swims around like a baby alligator. He then places himself along the top of the trough to sunbathe and dry off. His long tongue flicks in and out as he sips the moisture. His home seems to be in a crevice in the wall on the lower terrace along with other baby geckos, shyer about interacting with us humans. They keep many of the hairy creepy-crawlies at bay.

I once saved a newly-born gecko. It was a dull translucent pink with dark eyes that were bigger than its body. It was scrambling around on the shiny surface of the cooker. How it got there I will never know. I deftly put a piece of card under it, followed by a wide-brimmed water glass on top. Gingerly, I brought her outside then removed the water glass and put her gently on the wall of the top terrace. She scrambled up to the ceiling and still lives to tell her tale.

A rather plump, salmon-pink, female gecko—well she looks female—appears at night on the lower terrace wall. One evening I found her in the small dressing room dashing in and out from behind pictures. She is a different breed to the others, an albino gecko, but simply Pinkie to me.

I was once about to perform my daily hose down of the roof of my car when I found a note on the steps. I picked it up and unfolded a grubby piece of paper.

It read:

Can we ditch the ballet-moving, fouling feathered newcomer?

She'll never love you as I do.

Your Ever Devoted

Martha

(Signed with a paw print in chicken poo)

Too late, too late, Martha.

Good news from Dilek. "You must take my offer of a second chicken. Mattie needs company," she tells us. We accept.

I plead, "Selma, can you speak with Ahmet to get a move on and build that promised chicken coop, please?"

Eclipsed

Dilek (Selma's friend and neighbour living further up the mountain) walked up the dirt track, a bowl of fresh eggs in one hand and under her other arm a timid white-and-grey speckled playmate for Mattie.

"Welcome to our village," Dilek called out as she placed the pullet alongside Mattie. Mattie did not engage with the little one. She continued in her quest to eat and seek out food. Martha, on seeing the arrival of another feathered creature, turns her back to us humans and sulks. I thank Dilek for her gifts. We drink çay as she relayed her wisdom on things fowl. Selma joined in with her lifelong experiences of rearing chickens on her father's farm. They then tutored me on how best to feed our growing family.

"Selma and I will help you Miriam." Dilek took my hand to reassure me, the naïve city girl. "My chickens are free to roam. We feed them only the best grain, no wheat." If you follow our advice and do the same, soon you will be eating your own eggs for breakfast."

It was time for her to return to her working day on the farm.

Mattie is a bit of a tomboy and can be stroppy. The newcomer seemed more aloof with a ladylike manner—we decided to christen her Beatrice. At first Beatrice was a nervous soul and bossy Matilda took advantage. She did not waste any time before initiating Beatrice on her first morning with a peck or two: 'Don't worry, you will soon get into the routine of how things work here. I am not sure what the lady of the house is feeding me but it is never enough. Just remember, I get first pickings! I was here first. I am of a higher ranking so that's only fair. No rushing in, know your place, follow me around and there will be no trouble.

'But be warned—watch out for the funny-shaped dog who responds to the name Martha. She does not like us feathered types when we are alive and moving. However that changes when the man CJ (who is more tuned in to animals) feeds her with one of our own... a whole cooked chicken carcass—can you believe it? Greedy thing that she is she eats the lot, starting by daintily picking at the smaller bones. Once she has demolished the whole bird, she lies on her back as if drugged, bottom half in her bed and the top half collapsed on the floor—spaced out after that monstrous meal with no guilt. I ignore her and I suggest you do the same. Glide the other way if she approaches, the moody old spinster. Thinks she owns the area always bouncing that heavy body around our new owners, the foreigners, always looking for their attention.'

Naughty, bitchy Matilda.

After a few days of adjustment these two are joined at the wing, firm friends as long as Beatrice adheres to Matilda's pecking order. They follow each other, or rather, Beatrice struts behind Mattie. Mattie continued to kick up a fuss when food was around pushing Beatrice out of the way at feeding time.

'Beatrice, remember to allow me to test the food first. Between you and me that Irish woman does not know what she is doing. You can tell she has never looked after our sort before. Yet her expectation remains that we will lay top-class quality eggs for her and the man as soon as we can. Just be friendly and clucky with her as she is the main hand that is feeding us for now.' Mattie struts off.

To keep me on my toes, Mattie has taken to tapping her beak on the window of my office. As if to say, 'Hurry up, you're late again with the food. It's all about the food...' as she tap-tap-taps on my window pane.

Cheeky bird.

In my old life friends and colleagues complimented me on my interior design and creative abilities both inside and outside the house. Little did I think I would be using these talents to design and help Selma's husband Ahmet build a chicken shack and run. He finally appeared with recycled bricks and tiles for the shack and wood and wire for the run. Beatrice and Matilda were now living in the lap of safe and sheltered luxury.

Dilek's and Selma's advice paid off. Soon Mattie and Beatrice were laying two of the most delicious bright-yellow-yoked eggs each morning. They are small and perfectly formed, proving eggs taste great when chickens are fed on a natural organic diet.

Whilst throwing food scraps to the girls Selma asked, "Miriam did you know that chickens eat scorpions?"

"No, I did not." I freaked out. "How and why?"

"Well, chickens will eat anything as you may have noticed. Scorpions love bugs of any description but if the chickens eat the bugs there is no reason for a scorpion to be around. That said, if a chicken sees a scorpion it will spear the stinging tail with its beak, kill the scorpion, eat the tail and then gobble up the rest of it in one mouthful."

"Agh, no, don't tell me... it's too much information... I don't want nightmares tonight."

Selma responds, "Well it's better the chickens do

the dirty work, otherwise you will have scorpions making their homes in every crevice and crack both inside and outside the house. By keeping chickens you have a natural pest control system in place with no nasty chemicals required to get rid of the scorpions." She seems to have relished sharing this information.

"OK, OK, that's enough Selma,' I say, putting my hands up for the scorpion/chicken lesson to finish. "Thinking about it, it is a positive thing to have chickens around. But what bits of the scorpion are in the eggs I am eating? Oh Selma, I dare not dwell on these facts because I need my protein breakfast each morning."

The terrible twosome set up a laying rota. We became accustomed to hearing their early morning laying calls. One protects the other by standing guard outside the chicken hutch so the other one, secure inside the hutch, can drop each egg into the soft nesting area.

Their scratching ritual as they search for worms, two steps forward and one back then shake your head, in which Beatrice and Mattie perfect a type of chicken line dancing is pure entertainment. They also created a dry dusty bath for themselves in the form of a large hole close to my car, in which they tossed and turned with a synchronised wave of their wings. They sat in this dry bath for hours on end.

Unknowingly, we created the *Pink Pines Retreat and Zen Spa for Chickens and Dogs*. Please... no more animals need apply, we were fully booked. Our newfound skills were being stretched to the limits with this demanding family.

As the mornings became brighter the dawn

chorus was busy rehearsing for the longer sunny days ahead. The fairies had been painting the mountains and valleys while I slept. I was surrounded by a landscape similar to an Irish, emerald green, infinity carpet. White daisies formed an infinite blanket across the fields thanks to the deluge of rain that soaked the land throughout the short winter months. Cornflower blue wild irises and lavish, creamy white and yellow roses had sprung into bloom and swayed gently in the breeze. Along the mountain roads lime-coloured balls of flowers appeared randomly, contrasting with the bright pink flowers of the oleander bushes. I woke each morning feeling refreshed. We were in the throes of this unique rebirth time of year. Spring had arrived.

With this season comes spring cleaning, executed like a military operation by the even more efficient Selma. Everything gets washed, scrubbed, vacuumed, cleaned, shaken, brushed, sewn or moth-protected. Windows and doors remain open all day, allowing the fresh, clean, pine air to re-energise each room in the house.

Although we relish this time of year there is a downside, an unwelcome visitor... a yellow fairy dust appears at night from the pine trees and covers every centimetre, in and out of the house, Martha's coarse thick coat and my car. My sneezing sessions take their toll on this body. We have to accept this coloured dust will finally disappear when the last of the rain comes to wash and dissolve it away.

At that point Selma retrieves her brushes, dusters and the water hose comes out again. How the Turkish love using water to hose and cleanse; it is part of the culture.

For days I spied the women of the village gathering leaves from the tops of certain trees. I asked Selma, "What are these women harvesting?"

"They are spring green healthy shoots," she replies.

"Ah, so that is what you surprised me with when you appeared with one of your home-cooked dishes a few nights ago." I tell Selma. I recalled eating this particular dish not knowing it was the village brand of laxative.

"We like to boil them au naturel (I would lightly steam them) or cook them with onions and garlic. We eat this healthy green food with vegetables, makarna*, salad and yogurt. We fill small bags and freeze them for the rest of the season." Selma explained. "Miriam, these shoots are filled with goodness, iron and vitamins. I have said before you must have a spoonful each day and you will never have to worry about being constipated. Why do you not eat more of this super, natural, green food?'

Err, for exactly the reasons you stated Selma, but how could I tell her that without upsetting her?

"Packed with" is usually the Western way of describing any food the big conglomerates wish to market and promote in the name of healthy eating. But if Selma says it is so, I'm happy to believe it's true. Who needs three to five Spirulina or Chlorella tablets a day when I can eat cooked leaves from the top of a tree? As I write, I see Selma up a tree picking a few more kilos of these shoots and then placing them into a large hessian sack. I know what is on her menu for dinner this evening and maybe another cooked dish of the healthy stuff will appear at mine tonight. Perhaps I need to eat more of this miracle food she raves about, to keep Selma happy and everything moving.

As the slow transition of Spring unfolded one day the unexpected happened.

It was around midday on March 29th, 2006. I sat on the terrace. Everything was wrapped in an eerie silence as the temperature dropped dramatically. An inky black skyline enveloped the village, daylight vanished, time seemed to stand still. Where was Martha? No sight or sound of the chickens, no birdsong. Alone, I drank my green tea. A few moments before I had felt warm in the blazing sunshine. Now, a chill coursed through my body as goosebumps rose on my arms and the hairs on the back of my neck stood up. What would happen next?

I put my cup and saucer on the table in front of me, sat back in my chair, took a few deep breaths and waited. I was regressed to the early hours of the morning, as if I had stepped onto a huge film set, everything lit up with the shadows of a full moon.

I saw Martha jittery and afraid under the table in my office. She lay on her mat and refused to venture outside. Mattie and Beatrice, with not a 'cluck' between them, were in their hutch.

I waited in this veil of mystery.

Many minutes passed, then a solitary bird sang—its sharp staccato song echoing across the landscape, just like dawn each morning. An ever-increasing chorus of birds gathered as they joined the solo birdsong. The sun reappeared and the heat of the day slowly returned as the sinister shadows disappeared, life resuming as if nothing wondrous had just taken place. I felt that I was waking up from a deep and dark dream.

I realised this was my first experience of a total eclipse.

Still in a hazy whirl my mobile rang out... I jumped. It was CJ.

"M I have to tell you what I have just experienced. Wow is all I can say—a miracle, a total eclipse. Did you witness and feel it too?"

"Oh yes, right here on the terrace," I replied.

"Well I am at your favourite lake in Koyceyiz (ku- jay-iz). It was surreal. I was parked halfway up the mountain with views down to the lake. As if I had flicked a switch, it changed from a bright blue calm mill pond to a dark grey piece of crystal glass. Not a sound for miles around. In truth, I felt quite spooked by it all."

He asked, "How are the animals doing?"

"As I speak they are undercover, frightened, pretending to be asleep. They have no wish to step outside." I answered.

Later, friends called to say they were sailing around Kas and Kalkan, about two hours east, to experience the eclipse. They regaled me with their tales and adventures.

"You should have been there. It was mind blowing," they exclaimed. "Being at sea made it even more incredible. How extraordinary how nature can change our surroundings in the blink of an eye," one friend said. "We'll never see anything like that again."

How right she was. The next total eclipse is due in Turkey in about fifty years' time. Even with my many elixirs, age-defying technology, miracle creams and positive thinking, I have a strong feeling I will be not around, unless of course I reappear in another form. Now there's a thought.

Three months in, we enjoyed eating the fresh eggs we collected each morning. We had grown fond of Mattie and Beatrice. Martha accepted her feathered companions by ignoring their quirky ways as she continued to get high by eating her cooked carcasses.

There was one aspect of keeping chickens I was not so keen on. I was tired of their ongoing pooing. I was left to clean and hose down the terraces due to their mess. It was a twenty-four-hour wipe up operation. I had become chief pooper scooper...

I had to ask the question. "Selma are you putting those green shoots and leaves in their feed or is this normal for chickens?"

"Miriam this is normal," Selma assured me.

That evening as I sat with CJ, "We have to make a decision, I cannot live surrounded by this poo mess any longer. Mattie and Beatrice have taken to eating my plants and flowers and throwing the soil on the terraces too. Enough." I say.

"I understand, but what a shame," he shrugs.

Next day as Selma throws our scraps of fruit and vegetables to the chickens I call out.

"Selma, what about you taking the chickens and add them to your flock? We could transport their house and chicken run to yours. We will pay for the grain food and in return we can still have the joy of eating fresh organic eggs each morning."

"I will speak with Ahmet. I think he will agree. If that makes you happier, yes, let's take care of Mattie and Beatrice for you. No more mess on your terraces. Just as well you are not rearing goats and sheep," she laughs. "Then the shovels would be in use all day long, not the simple spray of a water hose pipe." She thinks I am being far too fussy.

And that is what came to pass. We remained proud owners of fouling fowl, but at a safe and cleaner distance... That is not to say that Mattie and Beatrice do not visit to say 'hello' every now and again with Mattie squawking for food—some things do not change. Neither does the mess they leave in their wake.

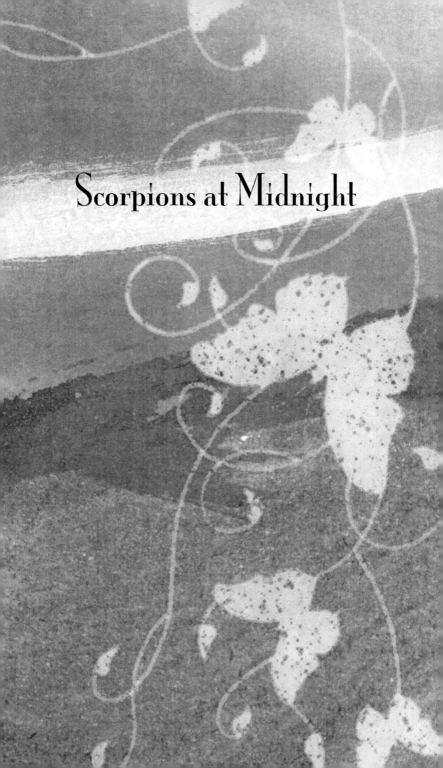

Scorpions at Midnight

"Success is yours for the taking over the next week in your work life and there is much excitement in your romantic encounters, but beware of a woman in black..." I stood in front of my audience which was listening with undivided attention. My one devotee, CJ (propped up in bed at the time), was enjoying his astrology forecast. I looked up, hoping for a deeper connection with him—only to spy, mid-sentence, a chunky, hard-shelled, black arachnid hanging out on the wall.

Oblivious to the danger behind him, CJ was insistent, "Well, don't stop just as you're getting to the interesting bit. I want to hear more about this woman in black."

I trailed off with the question in my head, 'Do I spoil the moment by announcing the bad news or do I finish reading his positive forecast?' I opted to finish what I had started while I kept one watchful eye on the black beast. With the good news relayed perhaps CJ was ready for the not-so-good news.

I whispered, "Darling, I need you to be really still. On the wall above the headboard behind your left shoulder is a black scorpion—don't move."

There was a mosquito net between the scorpion and CJ, but, if it felt threatened, the net would not protect him. CJ is a man of a measured disposition when handling tricky situations. On this night however all composure flew out the window... Resembling a freak flash of lightning, CJ jumped out of bed.

"Christ M, how can you stand there reading my horoscope in your calm voice knowing my absolute pet hate is looming behind me? She could have decided to sting me. Jeez M... Shit!"

I tried to calm the situation, "CJ, there's no need to make a fuss, just as you tell me. Compose yourself and move slowly. As it happens you have not disturbed Ms. Beasty, she is still hanging in the same place. Obviously she quite likes your side of the bed... and wall."

Panicked, CJ disappeared into the kitchen before returning with a small, wide-brimmed glass and a piece of flat card. With a steady hand he managed to trap the scorpion. He placed the glass over the black beast and put the card between the glass brim and the wall. The scorpion dropped into the base of the glass, sealed away from harm, the card firmly on top.

"M, that was a close call." Flushed, with beads of sweat on his forehead, he nervously went outside. I followed as CJ walked to the edge of the lower terrace and threw this black lady into the darkness of the forest.

Back in the bedroom he was still perturbed by the incident. "Come on, let's recheck inside the bed covers and underneath the bed for any more stray members of her family." We did so, thankfully without encountering any more black-shelled surprises.

"So much for the positive astrology prediction. That must have been the warning about the woman in black." CJ smiled and seemed more relaxed... but the remainder of his good news was quickly lost and forgotten.

A few weeks later we sat on the top terrace, sticky after a long hot summer's day, waiting for the cool breeze. When it came it flowed down through the forest enveloping us and helping us breathe more easily again. The moon slowly made its golden dramatic entrance into the night-time sky as it appeared over the top of the mountain. Crickets chirped and owls hooted under the stars as we cleared away the remains of our evening meal and prepared for bed.

Barefoot, CJ carried a full tray as he walked in and out of the house. Mesh-covered doors and window frames are essential as insect deterrents. Without them, with temperatures over thirty-five degrees, there is an invasion of strange flying bugs and multitudes of crawlies cross the threshold. Mosquitos, multi-coloured moths and flying ants will appear, many of them eager to bite or sting their human prey.

From day one at Pink Pines a critical rule was put in place, passed on to us by Selma and Ahmet: "Do not walk in the dark without wearing appropriate footwear, even in the house... Do not walk around in bare feet, full-stop!"

Ignoring the first rule of village living CJ carried on in his bare feet, with me tut-tutting. "Oh, I'll be OK. I know where I am walking and what to look out for," he replied.

Not clever, not smart, as the varnished wooden floors have dark patches which make it tricky to see any crawlies or stinging insects in the night hours of shadowy light.

I was propped up in bed quietly reading, lost in my peaceful, pre-sleep zone when, without warning, the peace was shattered by an almighty roar coming from the lounge... followed by much cursing.

"Oh, my toe, my toe. I have trodden on something with a shell. I have been stung! Oh, the pain, the pain," CJ called out. Reluctantly, I got out of bed and walked into the lounge where, to my horror, I saw that my husband had managed to step onto a large crunchy creature. At first we thought it was a hornet wandering around the floor (they are also known to administer a nasty sting), but no, there were no yellow stripes on this fella's back.

On further inspection it seemed nature had decided to teach CJ a lesson. There on the ground was another black scorpion. It had targeted his big toe on his right foot. Swearing, wailing at full pitch, CJ hopped around the room like a madman, angry at his foolishness... Within seconds, having delivered her attack, Ms. Scorpion was gone like a puff of wind. She had scuttled off, escaping under the mesh door into the wilderness and the moonlit night.

I asked myself if it had been the same scorpion CJ had thrown into the forest some weeks before returning to seek its revenge.

"We have got to get you to the local hospital for a serum injection now," I said. Without delay I threw some clothes on, grabbed the car keys and some bottled water, then headed out the door. CJ, hopping on one foot in my wake, was muttering through his pain.

"I'll drive," he moaned, "it will take my mind off this horrendous stinging." With some manoeuvring in the dark he eventually got himself into the driving seat. In great discomfort he drove down the mountain jerkily, howling like an injured pup every time we hit a bump or pothole. We drove past a handful of isolated houses, all in darkness. CJ's strangulated screams echoed through the open windows and sunroof into the otherwise silent night. I felt for the house dwellers, abruptly awoken from their deep slumber fearing that they were under attack from some wild animal.

On arrival at the small local hospital, we were met by two friendly nurses, "İyi akşamlar." They smiled as if to say, "We have been waiting for you." They directed us inside the main doors to an emergency area where a table, a bed and a screen awaited us. Looking to me they asked a few questions in Turkish, among them, "What happened and when?"

I pointed to CJ's toe. They both looked down at CJ's foot, now redder and swollen. I did not have to explain or give many details after that.

One of the nurses disappeared behind a curtain only to reappear with a young doctor by her side. In excruciating pain, his toe throbbing, CJ could hardly speak. The perspiration dripped from his hairline (and his pink bald patch) onto his face. I explained to the doctor, "He has been stung by a scorpion; he must have immediate medical attention."

The friendly nurses took charge of their patient, "Mister CJ, can you please get onto the bed face down and take your trousers down."

Husband was about to follow these instructions when he realised that having being so hot and humid, never imagining he would be in this precarious situation at such an hour, he was dressed commando-style. He quietly shared this information with me.

I was barely able to contain the news as I erupted into hysterical laughter.

For some form of modesty to prevail, I asked, "Pardon me nurses, out of respect for you, may I have a medium towel to cover my husband's rear end please?" One of the nurses promptly produced a thick towel and I put it in position. Adding to the even greater heat of the moment I saw CJ was lying on a plastic covered bed. This produced even more giggles from me. Not the kind of caring and loving wife CJ needed at that precise moment.

Both nurses smiled and under instruction from the doctor filled two large syringes to inject into each of CJ's cheeks. CJ, his head down, eyes closed, teeth gritted, had no idea of what was going on behind him.

I whispered to the nurses, "Please do not inform my husband about the injections. Just do it, it will be over before he realises what is happening."

CJ's other worst nightmare, despite being a doctor's son, is a total fear of injections. He comes out in a cold sweat if he sees the eye of a needle. The nurses stood, facing CJ's covered derriére with him facing the wall with his head down, counted down and in went the needles long and deep.

"Aww... Ouch that hurts. What the..." CJ cried out.

"Breathe short breaths as if you are having a baby," they instructed him.

He managed to cry out, "I have never had a bloody baby." The not-so-calm superhero was now super-distressed. My heart did go out to him, but I still could not contain the laughter. I put it down to the shock at being out at that hour of the evening and great tiredness.

"I cannot believe you are so lacking in empathy, you my wife and indeed the nurses too." He was feeling oh so sorry for himself.

Wanting to seem sympathetic I said, "Now come along CJ, the nurses mean you to take shallow, short breaths as if you were whistling through rounded lips. Push the breath out like a shush-shush-shush sound."

His response is not for this page... but it caused the nurses and I to look at each other with amusement and triggered more uncontrollable laughter from me.

Feeling unsupported and hardly able to move after the spasms from two intramuscular injections, CJ complained, "Jeez M, I don't know what is worse, these injections or the bloody sting."

Nursing his bright red, swollen toe, CJ managed to lift himself off the bed and get dressed with help from his devoted wife...

"Bravo Ms. Miriam for knowing to bring your husband here quickly," the doctor announced. "Mr. CJ you are a lucky man—that you were only stung once and not stung by the yellow scorpion... It is called 'Fattail'. In the past people have been known to die from these stings. Thankfully, with modern medicine, now we have the facilities to treat patients. It is no longer fatal but must be treated quickly. The patient can recover with no after-effects by remaining in hospital until the poison has been removed from the body. Here is the prescription for tablets and cream, one tablet for pain relief and the other to help the swelling go down."

Then one of the nurses turned to me, "Ms. Miriam, you must buy this cream now, rub it gently onto your husband's toe three times a day. Mr. CJ, please keep your leg raised. Do not put any weight on your foot for a few days until it feels comfortable again. If there is no change in the next forty-eight hours you must return immediately." As we left they chorused, "We wish you a good recovery."

We thanked the medical team and, with great effort, CJ stepped outside into the heat of the jasmine-scented night linking arms with me as he hopped along.

I drove with caution along the narrow road and parked. It was time for me to find the pharmacy. It was after midnight when I stepped out of the car and left CJ to lick his wounds and ponder his state of wellbeing or lack thereof... With a torch and a little overhead street lighting I made my way along the ghost-ridden cobble stones to find the duty pharmacy. Without delay the sleepy pharmacist issued the tablets and cream along with the same instructions given by the nurses.

Back in the car I took to the wheel, headlights full on and gingerly drove up the mountain with the occasional roar from CJ. As we chugged along the rocky road that led us back to Pink Pines CJ leaned forwards staring out of the windscreen.

"Am I hallucinating? Is it the mega injections or the fever that can come with a scorpion bite? I have not hit the raki bottle or indeed pulled on some strange herbs and tobacco from the hubble-bubble pipe but I could swear a group of four, long-legged animals resembling miniature baby kangaroos have just hopped in front of the car."

I had already spotted these alien four-legged animals, "CJ you are not delirious from the after-effects of the evening. You have indeed seen funny looking rabbits crossing our path," I confirmed.

I drove at a slow pace when suddenly a warm haze descended over us. What a weird night of calamity.

Arriving into the carport, lights on, Martha awoke to the sound of the engine and appeared at the office door. She was happy to see us, waggy-tailed, and set to go walkies. With a few hugs and gentle words from me she settled back into her soft bed and crashed out again.

It was a different story above stairs. As CJ hobbled to bed my first responsibility, as the newly appointed nurse, was to prepare a pot of calming camomile tea served with a few oat biscuits and honey for the shock. It seemed my next days were mapped out as superhero's nurse—a challenge at the best of times.

He swallowed the first two tablets. "Oh, I hope we both get some shut-eye tonight, don't think I can take much more of this burning and discomfort,' he said wearily.

My second duty was to ensure there was nothing heavy resting on his scorpion-stung foot. So I placed a light cotton sheet above CJ's ankle. The night dragged on. Each time CJ dozed off, his toe still throbbing, there was a piercing sound from his side of the bed. I was disrupted as he turned this way and that in his attempts to get comfortable—without success.

Nursing duties resumed before seven the following morning. With loose clothes on, CJ made his way out to the balcony and threw himself onto the rattan sofa where I served him breakfast on a tray. He insisted on some well-placed padding under his derrière and I produced a footstool with a soft cushion to support the toe which by then looked decidedly purple.

There he remained for the rest of the day with his laptop and mobile as he sought to work. With as much sympathy as I could muster I did what needed doing because of that intangible thing called love.

CJ is not a good patient and as each dart of pain came he continued to call out in rasps of impatience. He would not let me near his toe to administer the cream. "No way are you coming near this toe today," he said angrily.

Martha was not happy either. Done out of walking with her master she decided to take her revenge by running up and down the steps barking at CJ. Then she pulled at his trainers by the laces and threw them down the stairs and played with them around the gritty shingle in the carport.

"You know this probably would never have happened if Mattie and Beatrice were still here. They would have made sure no scorpion got inside the house," I heard CJ say.

'Ha', I thought... 'Far be it from me as the lowly nurse to mention the fact that this could have been avoided.' Welling up with anger I wanted to say, 'Don't be ridiculous man, if you had worn the obligatory covering on your feet you would not have caused yourself or me this distress.' I remained silent with my opinions, telling myself the man is delirious and in pain, so go with it for now M.

After thirty-six hours a miracle happened. The pain-relief angels appeared and took the stinging sensations, the swelling and the redness of said stung toe away.... well almost.

Within three days CJ was able to walk again

and our much needed quality sleep returned at Pink Pines. Most importantly, Martha was thrilled to have her master back—once I had retrieved his trainers, by then filled with dust and stones, from halfway down the track. He was able to take her for her early morning walkies. With the scorpion tale having a happy ending I was happily released from my nursing duties, grateful to resume my normal writing life.

Selma has since been able to solve the mystery of the funny baby-kangaroo rabbit-like animals, "Miriam, they are extra-long-legged hares only seen in groups late at night and they can run up to seventy miles per hour."

I am pleased to report that CJ has since taken to wearing his red cape with a more confident swagger again, with protective footwear in place... at all times. A lucky escape for my superhero.

A Dentist of Note

I was floating in a pink bubble of pure sound, lost in Russell Watson's voice as it washed over me. In my ear I heard, "Miriam s.. pee.. t please s.. pee...it...," the voice male.

My dreamlike state was broken as I was elevated towards the ceiling. My face felt numb, I blinked. In front of me a bright light beamed into my open mouth, to my right a smiling mouth of glistening pearly-white teeth. A man of tanned skin and bright blue eyes was talking to me while pressing a button on a machine, lifting me higher and higher. I felt that this was taking *You Raise Me Up* a little too far.

"Rinse and have a drink, Ms. Miriam." The gentle man pointed to a little sink of swirling water at my left where a cup rested beside the tap.

I was stretched out on a slippery pearly-pink reclining bed.... Reality kicked in. I was in a dentist's chair and before me the famous Tarkan. He of dentist fame as opposed to the award-winning pop prince of the same name. Tarkan, the pop star, is likened to a young handsome Elvis Presley of Turkey and is famous for his international hit *Kiss Kiss* his original song being *Şımarık** in Turkish.

I lay back on the recliner again as a button was pressed to lower me down for Mr. Tarkan to weave his dental magic. I closed my eyes as he put a narrow tube of water spray in my mouth while he commenced drilling with his fine drill.

Bathed in bright yellow light I closed my eyes and allowed my thoughts to drift right back to the first visit to this unusual dental surgery, more than three years before.

It was a sunny summer morning when I drove to

meet my new dentist in Dalaman. I arrived early, knowing I would have to ask for directions to the surgery.

I headed to my favourite bakery and çay shop for help. Sibel, the friendly owner, once the pleasantries of the day had been made looked at me, puzzled, when I asked, "Sibel where might this new building be?"

"Miriam, I have not heard of this new dentist. Please sit, have a Turkish tea, while I check with my friend the jeweller. He knows everyone in Dalaman. She left and the tea arrived as I sat under the awning in the sun. I saw the jeweller running out of his shop and then going into another shop with an insurance sign above the door. A tall man, who did not look Turkish (no thick black moustache), appeared and shook hands with Sibel. They walked across the road together and took a seat opposite me.

"Merhaba, nice to meet you. I am Tolga," the insurance man said. "What language would you like your directions in? I speak French, English, German or Turkish." As he spoke he puffed his chest out proudly.

"Oh, let's try French today," I replied, "once upon a time it was my second language. Je voudrais parler Francais s'il vous plait. Merci mille fois monsieur pour les directions."

With animated hand gestures Tolga gave directions, funnily enough, in Turkish—neither fulfilling his desire to speak another language nor my suggestion of speaking French. "It is a hundred metres from here on the other side of the road. There is a big sign over the entrance." He assured me, "You can't miss it."

I finished my tea, shook Tolga's and Sibel's hands, thanking them both for their help. I crossed the road and arrived at the fruit and vegetable shop to be told by the owner, "Doktor Dent is next door," pointing upwards with his forefinger.

To my left, with a large black and red sign over the entrance, was 'Doktor Dent'. How could I have missed this four-storey modern building in the heart of Dalaman? Somehow I hadn't even spotted the imposing smoked grey-green glass or the giant Turkish flag which hung outside one of the open windows, or the colourfully painted logo—a bright green, yellow and red coloured giant tooth lying on its side on a beach wearing sunglasses under a palm tree—with the words 'Diş Hekimi*'.

I entered the building, noticing a lift straight-ahead which would take me to the third floor. Instead, I climbed the stairs to stretch my legs as if to prepare myself for a Turkish-style check-up.

Huffing and puffing I arrived into what I can only describe as a Hollywood set for VIPs. Large double doors opened into stylish reception rooms with soft leather sofas that could easily swallow you up. A purple, velvet-covered chaise longue invited me to lie down and relax while I waited for the call to the surgery. Full-length floor-to-ceiling windows stretched across the room with panoramic views to the hills and Dalaman Airport.

I sat in a straight back chair for back comfort and waited.

A friendly uniformed dental nurse appeared. "Ah, you must be Ms. Miriam. We have been expecting you. Would you like tea, coffee or a fruit juice while you wait for Mr. Tarkan?"

"A glass of water, please." I reply.

The dental nurse reappeared, this time carrying an embellished traditional metal tray. She set the water down, "I am Mr. Tarkan's assistant. My name is Melisa, or in English we say sweet or charming..."

"Merhaba, Melisa, nice to meet you—I have to say you are exactly that—thank you."

She blushed with a "Mr. Tarkan will call you soon. Would you like a magazine, gazette or maybe you just want to relax and look out at the views from up here?"

The calm setting and the hospitality blew me away. I felt as though I was in a six-star hotel. For a moment I forgot I was awaiting a dental check-up in a working town in southwestern Turkey.

As I waited and sipped my tea a young man came into the room. He was long and lean with a shaven head and bright blue eyes that bulged. He wore baggy-arsed beige linen trousers and a wide kaftan that hung from his body. He looked weary as he pulled off a guitar which rested on his back and threw himself onto one of the chaises longues, his open-toed sandals hanging over the edge. Assuming he too was a patient I nodded and he smiled. He closed his eyes and remained completely still.

The call up to the surgery came, ten minutes later, via Melisa.

I walked with her up another flight of stairs. To my left was an open door with a fire escape, two fold-up stools and a small table set on the top step as the sun warmed the entrance. As I turned right I noticed the young man following behind.

We stepped into the pristine room. Immediately the young man ran to the man whom I could only assume must be my dentist, Mr. Tarkan.

"Baba*, Baba, I am home at last," the young man cried out. They hugged for a long time, sharing words of endearment I did not understand.

I stepped back at these personal tender moments, only for the older man to beckon me forward.

"Good Morning, Ms. Miriam, you found us at last. Welcome, I am Mr. Tarkan, call me Mr. T. This is my eldest son Zefir, he has just returned from Nepal after many months away."

My new dentist moved towards me walking with a limp. His handshake was strong. He is a small, thickset balding man, his eyes kind and caring. Between my average Turkish and Tarkan's few words of English we started to make conversation. I felt safe in this environment. Zefir warmly shook my hand too, his energy spiritual, renewed—he resembled a Buddhist monk without the orange-coloured garb. An emotional Zefir eventually leaves to find his mother.

I looked around the room, its décor was minimalist with mirrors, chrome cupboards and green glass worktops. In the centre was a peachy-pink reclining chair. On the wall hung a large, framed photo of Marilyn Monroe, her red luscious lips blew kisses from a blinding, whiter-than-white, set of teeth. In front of me were floor-to-ceiling, wall-to-wall windows.

I have attended many dental appointments in my western world in Blighty but never on this majestic scale.

The only flaw in this otherwise perfect room was a large, dirty, unpainted square where once an air con unit hung. All that remained was grey flaking paint and scruffy lines.

I had to ask Mr. T, "Why do you require such a vast space to work from?"

"Well Ms. Miriam, I have worked in dentistry in my own practice in Istanbul and as a professor to students and dentists alike for over thirty-five years. I have spent time in Germany learning about new technology and techniques to ensure I am up to date in all things dental. My plan is to develop this great building as the only dental hospital in this area and beyond where Turks, tourists and expats alike can feel safe; confident they will be looked after and have pain-free healthy teeth. I will bring students and dental nurses from the rest of Turkey to train here and I plan to have a research department too. My future students will go and spread the good news of what I am doing in this little town."

That certainly answered my question why he had acquired such a grand building.

"What exciting plans you have Mr. T, you are indeed reaching for the sky," I congratulated him. "But why this part of the world? Why not stay in Istanbul or live in Germany?"

"Life is at a quieter pace, I enjoy the clean healthier air. Much as I love Istanbul I only wish to visit for short periods of time now I am getting older, it is overcrowded and there is too much pollution," he replies.

"My wife's family come from further along the coast. You will meet with her later. For many years her wish has been to pursue again her love of, and passion for, all things equestrian. We have acquired a stud farm nearby to breed Arabian stallions for dressage and show jumping. Whatever my wife wishes I must do my best to make it happen and continue to make her happy too," he concluded.

"Mr. T, I wish you success in what you and your wife wish to achieve."

Would the people of Dalaman accept this city man who was modern in his approach to all things dental?

And so my check-up began with great ceremony as I was assisted onto the pearly-pink chair in an almost prostrate position.

"What music would you like to listen to?" Mr. T asks. "If you prefer I can set up the screen in front of you to watch a concert of your favourite group or pop band while I work on your teeth?"

Again blown away, this offer threw me off-kilter. "Music, concerts?"

"What about some Ser-ahhh Britman or Tarkan, our famous Turkish pop star. I can play more traditional Turkish music, Coldplay, Snowplough you name it we have it here. I even have well known Irish bands U2 or Chris de Burgh, Lady in Red. For me I enjoy old-style Celtic music, they are my favourite." He beamed. "I have surround sound and up-to-date technology thanks to my sons Faruk and Zefir who are both starting out in the music business studying everything that is available to be successful." He laughed as he swept his hand over the room showing off minute chrome speakers, gadgets and units I knew nothing about...

"Oh, ummmm... Well, let me think, what about a Riverdance DVD? That will soon take my mind off teeth." I replied, not thinking for one minute that he would have it in his archives.

Mr. T pressed a few buttons and, within seconds,

Michael Flatley made his dynamic entrance. He jumped onto the stage with tapping toes of steel—I had never seen such screen clarity.

Eventually Mr. T got to the task of the day, examining my teeth with sweet Melisa at his side. Her pen was poised as she prepared to write down descriptions of each tooth and his instructions on a flip chart. I gazed out at the undulating mountains and natural landscape as he infiltrated my mouth with various metal devices. The group of Irish dancers' tapping gathered momentum, all in sync. I was almost drawn to jump off the bed and dance to this mesmeric steel rhythm on Mr. T's marble floor when I heard, "Stand up, please." Mr. T led me to an X-ray machine to photograph the troublesome molars.

The results appeared instantly on a computer screen. We discussed the work which was required and made another appointment. We shook hands; Mr. T bowed and thanked me for my custom.

Before I left I asked Mr. T about paying my bill.

"Please follow me," he requested. I walked behind him as he slowly limped down a narrow corridor leading into a dark study of magnificent proportions. Opulent mahogany furniture and vases filled with red and cream silk flowers fill the room. Taking pride of place in the corner is an antique wooden desk, inlayed with green leather and decorated at the edges with gold. On one wall hung a full-length framed picture of Kemal Ataturk— who fought for the independence of Turkey and became its first President. To his left an even larger photograph featured a young Mr. T smiling broadly as he holds his graduation certificates.

"Ms. Miriam, I will open a file for you to record all the work we will do over the next months. I would rather you pay me in cash after each visit if that is agreeable with you?" Mr. T stood tall behind his desk, a gold pen in his hand.

"I am happy to do so," I replied, and after paying him we shook hands again.

Melisa appeared at my side and insisted on guiding me up another set of stairs to a sheltered roof terrace. Here I am introduced to Tarkan's wife.

She did not speak English.

"Ah Miriam, we meet at last. I am Suna, Welcome to our dental hospital. Please have something to drink, we are preparing lunch, Mr. T and my newly arrived son Zefir will come soon. Why not join us here on this terrace?" She stretched out her arms and embraced me warmly.

With both my face and gums still numb, and overwhelmed by the extensive hospitality, I found that I was unable to speak.

Suna was friendly and oh, so, pretty—blonde, brown-eyed with clear, healthy, olive toned skin. She was dressed from head to toe in a white ensemble: pedal pushers matched with an ornate, embroidered, short kaftan and matching bejewelled, white and silver shoes. Her nails are painted and her long light fingers carry dazzling diamond jewellery. Being a dentist's wife her teeth were perfect, white and sparkling, just like the rings on her fingers.

She called to her assistant "Bilge, please can you prepare some fresh Turkish çay for our guest?"

It seems that visiting my new dentist was a time for unwinding, socialising and an opportunity to be pampered.

Suna showed me to a white, rattan rocking chair. I listened to the sound of the birds whilst watching the occasional plane land or take off at Dalaman Airport. The çay appears, again on an almost regal Turkish tray, with a glass of water.

I find my voice, "Suna, please accept my apologies, I will not join you for lunch today. It is almost time for me to head home." I rose to leave the peaceful terrace.

Suna was disappointed, "Miriam, you must come again. We are eager to become acquainted with you, to learn more about where you come from in Ireland and why you came to live in this part of Turkey. As you know, Miriam, you Irish are famous for your jockeys, horse breeding and race meetings. I know this as my stable manager is from Ireland, Cork. I cannot understand his singing accent so we laugh a lot. You will meet him one day when you visit the stud farm. His name is Fin….Tan. Murr…fi, pardon it is difficult for me to pronounce this Irish name." She took my hand, a gesture of friendship.

It was time for me to leave, not quite believing my surreal morning in the clouds.

Over the next three years I continued to make the drive to Mr. T's practice. The ongoing work involved root canals, crowns and fillings as well as discussions of veneers that may be needed in the future for my front teeth, top and bottom.

From having perfectly healthy teeth it went pear-shaped when my immune system became so weak all those years ago while I was struggling to find a diagnosis as to why I was so ill.

Now I was paying a high price to rectify the tooth

situation I found myself in.

I was grateful to Mr. T for tuning in to my sensitivity and my energy levels; he did the work in stages and at the times that suited me. Once, when I was bleeding uncontrollably and in chronic pain, he opened his surgery at nine at night and on another occasion he insisted I see him one Sunday morning for a check-up or 'Kontrol*' as they say in Turkish. Normally Sunday was a sacrosanct day for him to spend with his sons and Suna.

Injections—I came to love them. I know, strange woman. The needles were so fine I never felt a thing as they entered my gum. I could have injections every day, feeling high with energy for a few hours and without a hint of pain when they wear off.

Even better, CJ/superhero became a patient and overcame his fear of needles thanks to Mr. T's gentle use of them.

One week into the final stages of bridging work Mr. T sent me a text,

Your bridge has arrived, can you come immediately please? Let's get it fitted so you can start to heal.

I texted him back;

Mr. T. my car is being serviced. I cannot come for a few days.

His reply,

> This is not a problem for me. I will send my son Faruk to collect you in my car. Be ready in forty minutes.

Forty minutes later there was the honk of a car horn below Pink Pines. I made my way down the marble stairs, whilst Martha threw a barking wobbly at the stranger on her territory.

I was chauffeured in a metallic-blue, convertible Mercedes the sun beating down with temperatures of over thirty-four degrees. Inside, I sat comfortably on cream leather upholstery feeling cool thanks to air-con. It was luxury all the way to Doktor Dent.

Once the bridge was fitted Mr. T offered me the usual opportunity to sit upstairs and drink çay with him and Suna. We were friends by then, meeting a few times a year to enjoy a Sunday Turkish breakfast over many hours at an oasis in the middle of the countryside. After this particular morning of dentistry I wished to head home.

Mr T asked Faruk to drive me home safely.

On our return drive the friendly twenty-something Faruk, a handsome darker version of his mother, asked, "Miriam what music would you like to listen to? Shall I put the soft top down?" He also informed me that we would drive the more scenic route back.

What is a gal to say when her mouth is filled with a new bridge and she feels numb? I just smiled and nodded.

The sun shone on my face as the scarf around

my neck blew in the light breeze. *The Ballad of Lucy Jordan* by Marianne Faithfull (the theme tune for *Thelma and Louise*), blasted out at full volume through the new high-tech speakers: "At the age of thirty-seven, she realised, she would never ride through Paris in a sports car with the warm wind in her hair..."

I was being chauffeured through Dalaman, high on injections with not a care in the world as Faruk swayed to the beat of the song.

"What made you think to play Marianne Faithful?" I asked through the booming sound.

"My father loves this lady and enjoys playing her music in the car. He tells me you are from Dublin and she has a house near there... So why not?" He smiled, one hand on the steering wheel and the other hanging out of the open window.

I could never have imagined the friendliness and hospitality at Doktor Dent. Life in Turkey, even in a dental surgery, was at a different pace than the West. With Mr T there was no rush or clock-watching, with him I witnessed the unexpected with many musical twists and turns.

Still tranquilised I am soothingly lulled back from my dreamlike memories of those last few years.

I am again in Mr. Ts surgery hearing his favourite words, "S..pee..t please, Ms. Miriam, s.. pee.. t." I open my eyes and look around. "Now rinse and rinse again," he orders me gently. "All is good with your bridge and teeth, there is no need to see you again."

"Thank you Mr. T. Can we make an appointment

for, shall we say, six months?"

"This is not possible," he tells me with a sad look in his kind eyes.

Confused, I ask why. "What about the new veneers for the top and bottom of my front teeth?"

"In one month's time what you see before you as Doktor Dent will be no more. I am leaving here to work with my sons as a promoter of international groups and bands. We are organising concerts on the biggest open stages in Istanbul and other big cities in Turkey.

I was reeling from this news, "But Mr. T, you said dentistry was your passion, your great love. What happened to all the big plans you had made?"

"Ah, Ms. Miriam, everything changes... even my dreams. I must help my sons in their future careers, they need me. They have invited me to join them on their journey to success with music in Turkey. As you may have gathered music is my other love and great passion. This is what I have in common with the famous pop prince Tarkan and my sons." He is animated and excited at the prospect of changing his career.

"If you wish you can come to Istanbul with Mr. CJ. I still use my old Surgery in Taksim—I can treat you there. I can also organise the best Concert tickets for you both, no problem," he wants to reassure me. As tempting as his proposal was to continue to live out this fantasy dental life... I knew I had to find a new dentist.

"What about Suna and her Arabian stallions?" I asked.

"Ah, her other love," he looks out to the Dalaman hills. "Suna will remain near Koyceyiz during the week to run the stud farm with Fin..tan Mr....fi, she will return to us in Istanbul each weekend."

Those surreal dental experiences were coming to an end but I shall never forget this man's care, skill and professionalism. A true craftsman. You name it and he did it with teeth. Life was transient again as Mr. T followed his new responsibility to perfect the careers of his sons.

I would miss: the quirky appointments, the social aspect to life at Doktor Dent, the buzz of the comings and goings in the surgery, the conversations with both sons and Suna, oh, and the various meetings Mr. T conducted with people whilst he continued to work in my mouth as I lay (oblivious) with my back to everyone.

'How shall I ever match Mr. T?' I muttered to myself. I was downhearted and sad at the prospect.

In reality it was time to seek out a dentist whose only interest was teeth. Maybe in the fullness of time I will blow kisses from a billboard, looking just like Marilyn Monroe, as people drive past in their cars and admire my perfectly-formed, gleaming white teeth.

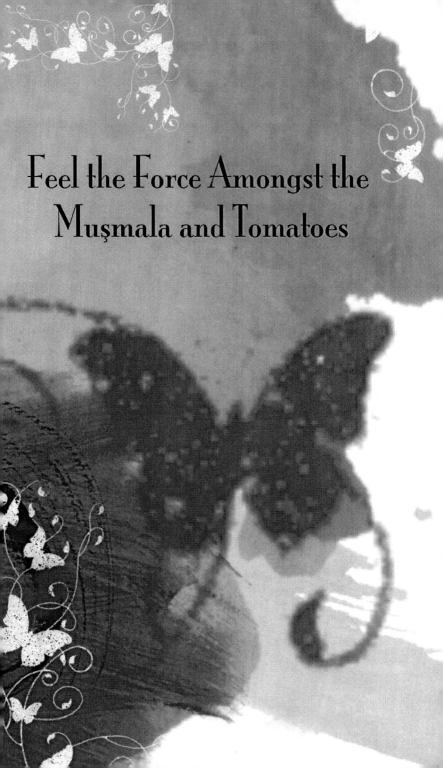

Feel the Force Amongst the Muşmala and Tomatoes

The sun rose over the red-tinged rock face. Birdsong filled the air on this steamy, hot morning. Cockerels crowed and a herd of goats with chiming bells competed with them. The shepherd led them down the valley to fields with more shade. There they chomp on whatever grass they can find in this dried-up dust bowl.

We bumped our way along the track as I drove nine kilometres down to the main road.

It's Sunday, it's Gocek market day.

We parked in the shade. CJ wanted to walk to the port and beyond while I did the market run. "So M, see you in about an hour at the Gocek Brasserie." We kissed and hugged as he set off. We were armed with large bottles of pure stream water.

The hub of the market is a long corrugated-iron-covered concrete area. Here groups of stallholders and their families have already set up their produce. Even though it was a hot steamy day ahead the stall holders still hoped they would have good business. The far end holds clothes, music, accessories and anything you may need for a home made out of wood, glass, plastic or linen. Some frayed makeshift fabric awning is overhead, giving the stallholders a little shade and hopefully protecting the mishmash of items for sale from fading in the scorching heat. A buzz of excitement flows through the market place—exchanges of neighbourly banter, the drinking of glasses of çay or the sipping of a salty, creamy frothy yogurt drink, the national beverage of Turkey, ayran. It is an acquired taste for us westerners. Normally served chilled with meat and rice, on hot summer days it helps to keep the body's salt levels balanced. The Turks seem to love it. Just as well, as in my experience, I do not see them drink much water. The market was awash with colourful seasonal fruits and the stimulating smell of herbs and spices filled the air.

Cherries, strawberries, apricots and peaches were all in season. Giant green and yellow-striped watermelons are displayed, some cut open to reveal their mouth-watering crimson flesh. They sit amongst fresh, crisp lettuces, large-leaved peppery rocket and small, aromatic sweet tomatoes on the vine. This fragrant, intoxicating atmosphere makes a refreshing start to my day...

An older man and his son stood behind a mountainous display of vibrant produce, offering cheery greetings in an attempt to attract customers. "Merhaba Sedat, merhaba Baba. How are you both?" I ask.

I have known 'Baba' and his son Sedat from our arrival in this part of the world. Baba did not mind when I christened him with this title. He reminds me of my grandfather in County Cork. He loved to get his hands dirty as he dug deep into the rich, dark earth. It produced the best organic vegetables, especially yellow-coloured potatoes.

Baba turned, squinting through his thick-lensed glasses the sides held together with black tape. His cloth cap was pulled down over his forehead, he was unshaven. His face lit up as he recognised me. He smiled, throwing out his big, muddy farmer's hands in a warm greeting.

"Welcome, welcome, come, come Miriam." Waving his massive hands in the direction of the shade behind him he says, "Come and sit with us. Please have a Turkish tea." Baba pulled out a few cracked white plastic stools at his side. A small wooden table was in place where breakfast awaited them, wrapped up in layers of newspaper to keep the food from drying out.

I accepted Baba's offer as it would be disrespectful to refuse his hospitality. I stepped up onto the platform to sit behind the vegetables, salad and fruit. I was surrounded by the pungent smell of freshly harvested garlic and onions that filled my nostrils, not good for a girl's tummy at that hour without breakfast. A small man, with freckles and greased-back red hair, swept past with a circular metal tray (similar to a cake stand) from which he served large steaming glasses of çay with, "İyi günler*".

'There's an Irish lookalike if ever I saw one. Pale skin, red hair with freckles. How did that happen?' I asked myself in wonder.

Baba sat with me, uncurling the newspaper to reveal fresh gözleme. There were also freshly baked simits*. A jam jar filled with honey sat on the side.

"Eat, you must eat with us," he exclaimed as he tore off a piece of gözleme, feeding me as one would a child. "My cousin has the gozleme and çay stand over there in the corner." He pointed. "She makes the best gözleme. the Turks and the yabancis will be queueing up later to buy them."

"Baba, do not feed me, I am due to meet CJ later to eat a traditional Turkish breakfast." I say this each week only to be ignored.

Baba shrugged and smiled as he took a big chunk of the pancake and shoved it in his mouth.

With that Sedat pulled up a stool and sat by my side.

"Miriam, I need your help to find a wife. I do not want to be alone for the rest of my life." Sedat looked at me with hope in his eyes.

Sedat is taller than many of the Turks I have met. He looks like a country boy, with a furrowed brow and weathered skin from the extreme conditions he works in. His dark, luxuriant, shoulder-length hair shone in the sunlight. Many a woman would kill to have that kind of glossy, quality hair. His eyes are dark and sultry, full of mischief. He is a friendly soul, polite and respectful to women.

I have seen him pick up, with his powerful muscles, sacks of onions or potatoes as if they were a simple bunch of flowers, throwing them over his shoulder to place them in the waiting boot of a car.

When I first visited the market alone Sedat would persistently ask, "Where is your friend, why is he not with you today" My reply was stern, "Sedat, respect please, that man you keep calling friend is my husband of many years. He is relaxing at home today. His name is CJ if you please."

A white lie, I was taking Selma's wise advice, "Miriam when you are out and alone always say CJ is at the house or is coming later. Otherwise the Turkish single men will take liberties checking to see if you are eligible for marriage. They will persist like the bees around the honeycomb. You have been warned."

Once Sedat met CJ he called him Aĝebey*, or older brother. Thereafter, he acknowledged me with the name of wife. He would take my hand, kiss it, then put it to his forehead as all younger people do as a mark of respect for their elders.

Back to Sedat's ongoing desperation to find that

ethereal wife of his dreams. "Miriam, when will you introduce me to your female, single friends? Surely you must know a lady from Ireland or England who would be happy to come and live with my father and I?

"I have much to offer a good woman. I have rich productive land. I have a house. She will have a good home with the best of food. She will live an outdoor life in the clean air of Koyceyiz—you know this part of the world near the magical lake you like to visit.

"She can learn about the markets with Baba and I. She can help to sell our produce each day. I do not mind an older woman who has good health and is not afraid of hard work. A woman who can bear children, a son for me I hope." He pleads.

Baba listens yet again to this conversation. With a quiver in his voice, "Miriam, as you know Sedat is my baby son. He is all I have left. I lost my wife many years ago. My other children moved away as soon as they could. They are all married. They live in northern Turkey or on the other side of the world. Sedat moved to Antalya when he was only eighteen to learn a trade as an electrician. He can do anything with wires and plugs.

"Sedat came back to support me a few years ago, leaving his friends and the woman he loved and hoped to marry. But she is a city girl. She runs a fish restaurant with her parents by the sea. She is not interested in a traditional country life. She does not wish to take care of Sedat or me.

"Miriam, I am over seventy. I am strong and healthy. I will not give up working my land or selling at the markets—this is my life. This is all I know. But I can only continue with Sedat's help." He held his head high.

"Sometimes it is a heavy burden to bear when you are alone." Sedat spoke in a low voice.

"There is still time for Sedat to find a good wife. He is only thirty." Baba slapped his son on the back and drank his çay with a noisy slurp. He wiped his mouth with the back of his hand.

"I will not give up," Sedat says as he walks over to rearrange his tomato display.

I listen to each of their stories with empathy, these two hardworking men who only have each other.

I stood too. I stepped down and walked back to the customers' side of the stall. "Taste the tomatoes, grown in the sunshine, I picked them from my garden at four this morning." Sedat leans over and chooses one of the beefy, fleshy fruits. He cuts one open with his sharp knife and hands me a piece. "Taste it Miriam, they are the best." Time to fill my bags with food and move on to my next destination.

I felt a tap on my shoulder. I turned to find myself looking up at a would-be, could-be wrestler or bodybuilder all six-foot-plus of him. A handsome, suntanned man with twinkly, deep blue eyes, thick white hair and a gentle smile. "Can you help me please? This is our first visit to a Turkish market. I have been observing you and how you interact with the stallholder. You seem to have a handle on the language and know your way about here. Are you a guide or translator from one of the big yachts? Do you get commission if you bring people to buy from certain stalls?"

I laughed... "No, I am not. We aren't that

commercially driven in this part of the world. I live here and I'm happy to help."

A crowd of curious people, all English-speaking, encircled the man and myself. "Let me introduce you to my entourage," the man said. "This is my wife, my friends, children and grandchildren. Oh, and I am Dave." This striking man shook my hand.

We nodded and smiled at each other.

The group spoke animatedly at the same time, asking many questions about me, how I came to live here, the area itself and the different Turkish fruit in season. Sedat, now excited, asked, "What is going on Miriam? Tell them how good our produce is. Will you translate for me what they were saying please?"

"Oh and find out if any of the ladies are single..." he asked, hoping his luck was in.

It was the apricot and muşmala season. The muşmala is shaped like a small, yellowish tomato. In Turkey they describe it as 'The New World' or an 'Atlas.'

I have only come to taste this fruit since living in Turkey. It is a brighter shade of apricot, topped with a green leaf. Taste-wise I remain a firm apricot fan. The muşmala is squidgy with a definite dry aftertaste. I know that Baba is an expert, his family have been growing them for over a hundred years.

My new friend, Dave, reached in and pointed to the muşmala, "Can we sample this interesting fruit?" he asked.

His family looked on as he bit into it. His nose crinkled, he made a distorted face as if to say 'not for me'. Another person who would have to acquire the taste.

"Which is your favourite?" he asked.

"I am an apricot girl through and through," I replied.

And so the fruit discussion carried on with lots of banter and humour. Dave tasted an apricot cut by Sedat. The family waited again for his opinion.

"Miriam, I am with you on that one." He started to fill a bag with kilos of the juicy, yellow fruit.

Sedat was delighted the group had bought from his stall.

My bags were now full and I paid and said, "Thank you Sedat and Baba, see you next week."

"No problem. We are here waiting for you." They meant it and waved me goodbye.

I turned to move on, Sedat calls after me, "Miriam, a small gift for you." He placed two lemons, a handful of carrots and a small melon into a bag with "Afiyet olsun". Such kindness.

Dave then asked: "Please, if you have time can you take us to the best cheese stall and tell us about the cheeses you recommend? By the way are you married to a Turkish man?"

"Oh no I am not," I say. "My husband is a mix of Scottish, Irish, English and Italian."

"That is quite a mix." Dave laughs.

I say, "Why do you ask?"

"It seems to me that you, an Irish woman, are fitting in well to life here. I can tell the Turks at the first stall embrace you and find you endearing."

"How observant, how sweet of you to notice."

"Well, as a writer it is important to be observant and curious don't you think?" He smiles down at me. "I love the Irish and how they weave their stories—do you write?"

"As it happens I do, Dave. I am passionate about writing. Living in this Eastern culture has been one helluva journey. Here I am, soon to publish my first book of short stories based on my adventures thus far in Turkey."

Dave spoke of how he was writing his memoirs and of his charity work with Phab. As writers we had a natural bond.

The entourage moved over to my 'cheese boys' as I like to call them. Their mobile deli sells cheese, butter, yogurt and olives in all shapes and sizes by the plastic-container load. Freshly baked village bread loaves are stacked high. Different types of helva*, a firm favourite of the Turks to eat as a dessert or drink with çay, are on display. They are hefty, big round circles of sugar and nuts which are weighed and bought by the slice.

The discussions continued as the families bought more food items from the cheese boys. Such an interesting and interested, friendly set of people.

Dave called to his wife, "Monica, do you have one of my business cards in your bag?"

"How about we keep in contact?" he suggested.

He handed me a big card with his photo on the front. I stuffed it into my handbag and we shook hands.

I said, "Happy holidays to each of you," as I turned to leave.

"You too Miriam, what a pleasure to meet you today. You've made it a memorable first day of our holiday. Thank you for your wonderful help. We will return. Let's meet at the same time, same day, at your fave stall on this very corner next year!" He laughed.

I waved them goodbye again (the Irish goodbye can go on for some time...). We wished each other good luck with the publication of our books.

With Sedat's help I carried my produce to the cool boxes in the boot of the car. Oh dear, I had been gone quite some time. I realised then how hungry I was. I was looking forward to sharing a traditional Turkish breakfast with my superhero and hoped he was still waiting for me.

I walked to the seafront, turning left onto the port. The sun was now high in the sky, a sticky heat that followed me as I slowly made my way towards The Gocek Brasserie Café which is, thankfully, in the shade.

"Jeez, M, where the hell have you been? I was about to give up. I'm afraid I had to start without you. I was bloody starving. Your blood sugar levels must be at point zero after that long trip to the market."

"CJ, you know what it is like in the Sunday market. As my grandmother used to say, "I went to the market and I met the world. Well it has been a bit like that this morning. Once I have ordered and eaten I shall tell you what happened to me."

"M, there is always a story when you go off on your own."

After a slow, lingering, power breakfast we walked back to collect my car. I drove back up the mountain to our peaceful retreat and we unpacked our fresh produce.

Later I pulled Dave's card out of my bag with, "Look, here is the photo of the man I met with his family today. He was a gentle giant, charming, with a great sense of humour." I handed it over to CJ.

He flipped it over, took a deep breath, and said, "Do you realise who you met today?" as he showed me a picture of a masked man in black costume armour.

"I have no idea. Who is he?"

Superhero looked at me in horror... "Are you saying that you never watched *Star Wars*, those iconic films? Surely you have heard of George Lucas or 'May the Force be with you.'"

"Doh... No, I have not. Sci-fi was never my thing," I replied.

Superhero laughed. "M, I cannot believe you have never heard of this character—one of the greatest movie villains in history. I cannot believe that you were chatting for over thirty minutes with the real Darth Vader. Worse than that, it was the one day—the one day—I was not with you." CJ tapped his head in disbelief.

"So my unknowing claim to fame is that I met Darth Vader or Dave as he is to me in his civvies. How would I have known from meeting him that it was Darth Vader—he always wore a mask? He came over to me. He stood out from the crowd with his distinguished looks and broad muscle-bound, fit bod and handsome features. As for thinking, 'Oh he must be a famous actor in an equally famous TV programme or film,' that would never have occurred to me."

CJ shook his head for days, upset that he was not there to shake his hero's hand.

May the muşmala and force of fruit be with you! May I meet up with Darth and his family next year at the same time, same place... for sweet samplings of fresh fruit in season... Oh, and may Sedat find that woman to share the rest of his life with—otherwise my life will be hell.

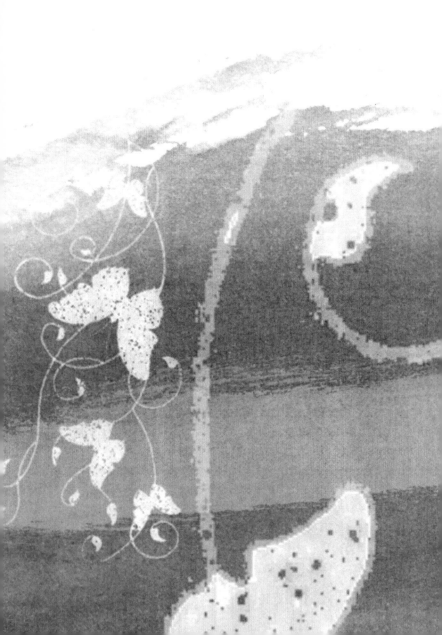

Magic Carpets
at
Pink Pines

We were enjoying a leisurely breakfast looking out to the panoramic views from the top terrace. This is our favourite time of day.

Martha was peaceful after our silent walk and lay stretched out, asleep at our feet.

Selma was flitting from room to room inside the house, gathering up our rugs and floor coverings at speed. She pushed through the squeaky, mesh door with each rolled-up piece of carpet. From the side of our breakfast table she flung them one by one, with great force, over the balcony.

I looked up and saw flying carpets whizzing over our heads. I tried not to wince as they landed in a heap with a swoosh and a thud on the terrace below.

In panic Martha ran from the upper, marble terrace and hid behind the rattan sofa. She appeared to be disgusted that her morning of after-walk recovery had been interrupted with such disturbing noise.

"Yikes, Selma what are you doing?" I asked.

"Miriam, it is too hot and dusty to have coverings on your floors. You do not want to find ants, crawling or even stinging insects setting up home in the wool or cotton fabric. This is the season to brush, wash and clean them." Selma sounded excited by the prospect.

This was not how we had planned to kick-start our day.

"Can this not wait until after breakfast?"

"I must get on with the job while the sun is up so the fabric can dry later." Selma was already walking down the marble steps. She unfolded each roll. She laid each piece out flat so that they formed a colourful Pink Pines mosaic on the stone terrace.

She disappeared, only to reappear with a stick and a natural bristle brush to beat the living daylights out of each rug. She brushed around and under the area where the carpets had landed earlier. A large basin was filled with warm water from several boiled kettles and from the cold water hose. After adding squirts of liquid olive soap Selma sprinkled the mix onto the carpets.

I was deeply concerned as my favourite cotton and wool carpet of teal, cream and red was about to get a soaking.

Selma looked up and smiled, "Don't be afraid Miriam, this is a stress-free, foolproof system."

She was reassuring me, the yabanci.

"I learned how to keep carpets dust and insect free when I was a little girl on the family farm. I watched and helped my mother and grandmother perform this task at the beginning of each hot season. I promise I shall wash and dry each one with love," she said. "Trust me, they will be cleaner than ever before."

What did I know of the cleaning rituals on such carpets? I accepted her plan to hand-wash my floor coverings.

In my old Western life I would telephone the carpet cleaning company and make an appointment for them to appear at some unearthly hour of the morning. The operation would take all day. The chemical smell lingered for days on end even when the windows were left open to clear the air. A lot of money changed hands for this service and I was never convinced that my carpets were any cleaner or fresher.

Back to Selma, who was working at full speed.

She called out, "Miriam, come down and join me. We can get fit by exercising together. All you have to do is slip out of your shoes and roll up your trousers above your calves. Then we can lightly jog on our toes up and down the carpets."

CJ was as perplexed as I was, "Trust our Selma. Go to it M, cleaning and cleansing in the sun."

"Selma, I have never in my life witnessed this way of cleaning carpets," I said, mesmerised.

"It looks as if we are crushing grapes," as I joined in the fun. "Oh Selma, if my girlfriends from Blighty could see me now... They would think I have finally gone over the edge with this mountain-living lark. For them it is a passing notion. Many still think I'll never adjust to these village traditions, that I will see sense and return to what they call real, high-heeled city life."

She shrugged, "That is their problem Miriam. If you are happy and healthy who cares where you live?"

"Keep jogging," she encouraged me. "We must ensure the fabric soaks up all the water." She was enjoying this lesson, showing me the how of this cleaning exercise.

The cool, soapy water was therapeutic as it ran through the gaps in my toes. I followed Selma as we moved up and down... and up and down, as I started to flow in rhythm with her.

"Once the carpets have absorbed the water, I must get down on my hands and knees." Selma told me.

That was my cue to take a break with a large glass of water while I sat in the shade of the low-hanging, yellow plum tree.

Selma carried on chatting as she revealed her knowledge about the history of handmade, woven Turkish carpets. "Miriam, carpets have been an integral part of Turkish history and culture even before nomadic times. The word 'kilim' refers to the way a carpet is made. Kilims are not just rugs for walking on. They have a range of uses; as tents, as luggage for travel and floor spreads for guests to sit on. They are even hung as coverings for doorways and walls to keep the cold draughty winds of winter at bay. I remember my grandparents using them in this way in their small simple stone house."

When the carpets were soaked to her requirements Selma started, with a soft scrubbing brush, to almost sponge the soap and water mixture together using long strokes up and down the fabric, then across the weave away from the pile. God bless her patience and energy. Now I know why she is fit and agile. Selma continued to hose down the carpets with more cold water until the soapy water completely disappeared.

When the water finally runs off clear, my feet and the terrace are left spotless.

Martha, still hiding, is not a lover of water. When the water hose appears it can only mean one thing as far as she is concerned... it will soon be time for her to get washed.

'How can I escape all this water?' Her face pleaded with me.

But it was too late... I retrieved Martha from her hideout and hosed and soaped her down until the hair on her back legs and tail were dust free. She enjoyed a treat of tasty dog biscuits while she dried naturally in the shade of an olive tree. Later that evening she would be brushed and groomed by CJ and me—all done with love.

Once Selma was satisfied the carpets were clean she rolled up each one inside out. She stood them up straight in the sun. "It will take thirty minutes for the water to drain off," she informed me.

Sopping wet, Selma looked as if she had been bungie jumping into a waterfall. The water dripped off her scarf; droplets shone and caught the sunlight from the ends of her jet black hair. She was glowing after such vigorous exercise.

"OK Selma, come on, time for you to sit in the shade, dry off and let us enjoy a Turkish tea with a glass of water. You can tell me more about Turkish carpet history," I suggested.

"Miriam, come to my house for çay one day. I will show you one of the carpets from my grandparents. I am the eldest child. They handed me these priceless pieces as a gift on my marriage to Ahmet. My grandparents originally received these vibrant patterned carpets from their parents. Like taking a large page from my family's past, I have placed my history on the floor of my house. When the time is right I will pass it on to my son. There are knotted patterns in each carpet, messages from my female ancestors." Selma was proud to impart this knowledge.

My Turkish history friend, Alif from Istanbul, had also relayed the secret messages of sorrow, death, love and terms of endearment that the female weavers of times past worked into the carpets with special symbols.

Alif unravelled this fascinating story as he escorted me to the carpet bazaar on one of my first visits to Istanbul, "Silk wall hangings and pillowslips were made for the opulent palaces in Istanbul and Europe many centuries ago. These handwoven rugs continue to be used as mats for praying or eating from. They are still used as storage bags to this day. In the twelfth century Marco Polo was so enchanted by the wool and silk fabric used to weave coloured kilims he wrote about them. He spread the word about these creative art pieces across Europe. Of course it was always the women who learnt the craft and the skill of weaving with symbols for each area."

There, in the bazaar, I heard the carpet traders tell their potential buyers, "Build a relationship with your carpets. They already have a life history passed down from one ancestor to another over hundreds of years."

'How?' I wondered... The carpet traders suggested that the buyer should hand-wash their purchase once or twice a year. That way they would get to know every weave and knot of the fabric of their carpet.

Now, thanks to Selma and Alif, I am able to acknowledge the tradition of the Turks who take off their shoes before entering a house or special building—so no dust or dirt enters from outside.

Once we were recharged, Selma and I unfolded the carpets and hung them over the balcony giving Pink Pines the appearance of a multi-coloured carpet bazaar.

"They must be left to dry overnight when the moon is up. Do not touch them until I arrive tomorrow morning," Selma ordered me gently.

Early the next day, she walked up our marble

stairs to check on the carpets.

"Finally, there is one more job I must do. This is another of the family's tried-and-tested methods of how to store your shaggy pile rug during the summer heat," Selma promised.

She dragged the heavy, goat, monster rug from the house. Again she threw it over the balcony onto the ground after ensuring it was brushed and vacuumed. She pulled out a bag of smelly moth balls from her pocket. I refused to let her use them.

"Selma, they are full of chemicals. They evoke memories of my grandmother's wardrobes in her home in County Cork where we had to hang our summer clothes." I shook my head. "You know I do not use chemical products on my skin, my clothes or anywhere in the house. Sorry Selma, I am sticking to my cedar shavings or cotton wool doused in cedar oil."

I collected the natural cedar from a cupboard in the house and threw it into the centre of the hairy, goat, damp-proof rug. Not convinced they would do the job Selma shook her head as she folded the shaggy pile in half. We repeated the exercise and folded the rug in two again. Selma rolled up the bulky rug. With my help she placed it in a large, recyclable plastic bag. Using some natural string we tied it up and then it was stored away.

Five months later I was very impressed. My shaggy pile rugs were smelling of fresh pine air. There was not an insect or hole in sight. They were in perfect condition.

"OK Miriam. I accept this new way of protecting your goat pile." We laughed as we continued teaching and learning from each other.

Selma brushed each of the clean carpets which by then were completely dry from the day before. Reluctantly she told me, "I have no wish to be the bearer of bad news—which is Eastern way. There are some tears on your favourite teal, cream and red carpet. It has thinned due to its age and the constant footfall."

"Oh no. I love this carpet. What can I do? I have no wish to get rid of it."

"Do not worry Miriam, I can fix these threadbare areas," she assured me. "I will go to my house and bring back coloured cotton, wool and my special needle."

When Selma returned we sat in the shade, she on a cushion on the ground, me on a comfy chair. Deftly she ran her needle back and forth, sometimes changing the needles as if crocheting or lace making. Once she had completed this mammoth task she held the carpet up to the bright sunlight.

"Wow, Selma my carpet is like new—thank you for upcycling it!"

With a look of mischief she asked, "As you cherish this carpet so much, what about I weave a few secret messages into it? You could write in code, a few simple words. No need for lovers' messages. I know you love CJ and he loves you." She smiled shyly.

I walked into my office and picked up a notepad and a pen. I wrote out a few words in Turkish for Selma. 'Peace, Calm, Love, Health' and the symbol for 'Ying and Yang' came to mind. Selma interwove her magic knots. İnşallah, my words will remain intact for many years to come, private, just between us.

I sat quietly reminiscing with Selma, "I have come a long way since first arriving here to find a new way of living and healing...."

I recalled many memories. Our first holiday by the sea, where a little miracle happened when I felt there was a light at the end of my long dark tunnel. The time I met my dear friend and confidante Deniz. Moving to our beach haven which I wished to be peaceful so I could swim each day and soak up renewed energy. The aggressive Serjan and the ever accepting Neglin, along with the Turks who did not wish to support us. This no longer filled me with anger or disappointment.

"Selma, I can honestly say I am changing. I have been given the gift of a calm, peaceful environment—I am truly grateful that CJ met Henry. I am letting go of what I thought I knew as an Irish Western woman. I realise your way of being and doing is working for me. I am growing stronger with each day."

"Miriam, I see this change, when you first arrived you were troubled, anxious, far too serious. Now you move at a slower pace, you are less impatient, you laugh a lot. That makes me happy."

"Selma, you have shown me only love by wanting to help and understand me. I am enjoying my simple natural life where gestures of goodwill far outweigh any material things I may have enjoyed in the West."

It was time for Selma to finish her job of work. She rolled up each rug, ready to store them away. Then she hugged me, "No going back now Miriam—

You are part of our family and life in this village."

"There is still much to learn," I say as she heads off to leave me alone with my thoughts.

CJ and I jumped off our western cliff in Blighty and landed in this piece of paradise. I wish to embrace, and learn how to weave and thread, the next chapter of my life on this magic mountain— the one I now call home. May it flow and blossom...

And maybe, just maybe, one day CJ will learn how to coordinate his left and right feet and dance rhythmically in his own Turkish way as he helps to clean my carpets...

Author Information

Miriam has turned her life around. Her motto: "You gotta do different to have different." She is passionate about writing, walking, swimming, yoga, eating locally-sourced food and adapting local recipes. Truly international this Irish (and proud) lady lives in Maidstone, Kent and south-west Turkey.

To stay up to date with all Miriam's adventures through her blog visit:

www.talesfromturkey.com

Miriam is active on Facebook, search for: Miriam J. McGuirk

Her twitter handle:

@Miriam_McGuirk

You can also find Miriam on YouTube and LinkedIn - all links can be found at

www.talesfromturkey.com

Other titles from mPowr Publishing

mPowr publishes a range of different titles including business books, complementary therapy manuals and fiction titles.

Here is a small selection from our current titles. These can be purchased from bookstores, online retailers or via mPowr Publishing's own online store at www.mpowrpublishing.com.

Don't Just Manage—Coach!
Ben Morton
ISBN: 978-1907282607

The Secret Medicines of Your Kitchen
Ellen Evert Hopman
ISBN: 978-1907282584

Bedtime Stories from the Woodland
Martyn Pentecost
ISBN: 978-1907282232

The Little Book of Celtic Reiki Wisdom
Martyn Pentecost
ISBN: 978-1907282669

Lightning Source UK Ltd.
Milton Keynes UK
UKOW04f0251160515

251660UK00002B/12/P